THE FIRST
NAVAL AIR WAR

THE FIRST NAVAL AIR WAR

Terry C. Treadwell

REVISED AND EXPANDED EDITION

SPELLMOUNT

First published 2002

This revised and expanded edition published 2010 by
Spellmount Publishers, an imprint of
The History Press Ltd
The Mill, Brimscombe Port
Stroud, Gloucestershire, GL5 2QG
www.thehistorypress.co.uk

British Library Cataloguing in Publication Data.
A catalogue record for this book is available from the British Library.

ISBN 978 0 7524 5881 6
Typesetting and origination by The History Press Ltd.
Printed in India
Manufacturing managed by Jellyfish Print Solutions Ltd

Contents

Introduction

There was not one single cause of the First World War – although many historians ascribe it to the assassination of the Archduke Franz Ferdinand, heir to the Austro-Hungarian throne, and his wife Sophia on 28 June 1914, by the Bosnian revolutionary student Gavrillo Princip.

Other factors played their part: colonial expansion, nationalism, envy, fear of neighbouring countries and ancient feuds set events in motion which proved unstoppable and resulted in years of carnage and the death of the flower of youth on land, seas and in the new dimension – air.

Of the fifty-seven nations who took part in the First World War, only fourteen had a naval air arm or a limited naval aerial capacity: Australia, Austria-Hungary, Belgium, Canada, France, Finland, Germany, Great Britain, Greece, Italy, Japan, Portugal, Russia and the United States of America.

These fourteen nations were aligned in warring power blocs as follows:

The Allied Powers
Australia, Belgium, Canada, France, Great Britain, Greece, Japan, Italy, Portugal, Russia (including Finland) and the United States of America.

The Central Powers
Germany, Austria-Hungary and Turkey.

Aerial warfare, as such, did not properly begin until the First World War although balloons had been used as observation platforms for nearly 100 years. The Italians used a Blériot monoplane, flown by Capitano Carlo on 11 October 1911, to reconnoitre and later bomb Turkish lines during the Italian-Turkish War. During 1913, the Spanish carried out observation, photographic and bombing sorties in Morocco.

During the Mexican Civil War, another attack using a naval aircraft was carried out on 30 May 1913. A Glenn Martin pusher aircraft of the Constitutionalist cause carried out an attack on the Federal gunboat *Guerro* at Guaymas in the Gulf of California. The handmade bombs missed their target completely, demonstrating that hitting a moving target from an aircraft was not that easy. The crew of the ship opened fire with rifles without hitting the aircraft, demonstrating equally that hitting a moving aircraft whilst under attack is not easy either. A second attempt, made one year later on the *Guerro* when it engaged the former Federal gunboat, the *Tampico*, was also futile, but it showed that with more practice there was a role for the aircraft against ships.

The First World War started on 1 August 1914 when Germany declared war on Russia and invaded Luxembourg the next day. On 3 August 1914, Germany declared war on France and promptly invaded Belgium. Great Britain responded to this aggression by declaring war on Germany on 4 August 1914.

Already the opposing blocs were lining up; Austria-Hungary declared war on Russia on 5 August 1914 and France declared war on Austria-Hungary ten days later. Two days later, on 12 August 1914, Great Britain declared war on Austria-Hungary. Japan joined in on

23 August 1914, aligning itself with Great Britain and France by declaring war on Austria-Hungary, who promptly retaliated by declaring war on Japan and Belgium. Russia then entered the war on two fronts by declaring war on Turkey on 31 October 1914. In support Great Britain also declared war on Turkey on 5 November 1914.

Six months later, on 24 May 1915, Italy declared war on Austria-Hungary, then over a year later, on 27 August 1916, they declared war on Germany. The same day Romania declared war on Austria-Hungary. Immediately Germany retaliated and declared war on Romania and, on 30 August 1916, Turkey followed suit by also declaring war on Romania. This was not the end of the declarations of war – on 1 September 1916 Bulgaria went to war with Romania.

The Austria-Hungary Naval Air Arm had its origins in 1909, when several of its naval officers were sent to Great Britain and France to learn to fly. Returning to their homeland these aviation pioneers laid the foundation of a successful naval air arm. At the outbreak of war the Austro-Hungarians had twenty-two aircraft at their naval air stations and were in action within days. At the end of the war they had 591.

The First Naval Air War had its beginnings early in the 1900s when several of the later combatants began to see the advantages of air power. The introduction of LTA (Lighter Than Air) and HTA (Heavier Than Air) vessels into the navies of the western world was one of those innovations that made the old guard recoil in horror. They didn't want change – the general sentiment was that the old ways 'had worked for years' and these flying machines were 'so fragile they wouldn't stand up to the rigours of naval life and the hostile elements that battered the ships whilst at sea, and in any case what use could they be?'

These were some of the reasons given to fight the introduction of aircraft into the navy, but fortunately the persistence of the more forward thinking members of the various navies prevailed, and experiments were carried out using a variety of airships, balloons and aircraft.

The Hall Flying School at Hendon in 1913. A number of RNAS officers learned to fly here before joining the navy.

It was soon realised that the rapid development of aviation was going to play an important part in the role of reconnaissance, and ships at sea would find the role of the aircraft invaluable in searching for enemy ships. The major problem facing those who wanted the aircraft introduced into the navy, was that the balloon, airship and aircraft were untried and untested pieces of war machinery – as it was with land-based aircraft and airships also. No one knew their potential as no one had used them in this role before. 'Necessity is the mother of invention' – the use of aircraft in the First World War epitomised this statement. The rapid development of aircraft surprised everyone, and within a space of four years aircraft had developed from the canvas-covered spruce wood of the Blériot, to the all-metal Junkers flying boat fighter.

The successful attack by seven 2F1 Camel aircraft of the Royal Naval Air Service from HMS *Furious* on the German airship base at Tondern, in which the Zeppelins L.54 and L.60 were destroyed, added great strength to the argument in Britain as to whether or not aircraft on ships would be a success. This was the first carrier-borne attack carried out by aircraft on an enemy land target.

On 6 April 1917 came the momentous declaration of war by the United States of America on Germany, thereby altering the course of history. The following day the United States formally declared war on Austria-Hungary. The war that had started in Europe had now cast its evil shadow over most of the civilised world.

In Germany the Imperial Air Force was making major strides in the development of their aircraft, mainly due to the Dutchman Anthony Fokker. It was the Germans who first introduced *Feldfliegerabteilungen-Infanterie* (infantry contact patrols) which in these early times and in the absence of reliable radios, was the only way commanders, on the land and on the sea, were able to obtain information of the enemy's positions and strengths. The introduction of photography, wireless telegraphy and automatic weapons during the war also gave the aeroplane a wider aspect of use and slowly, if not somewhat reluctantly, it was realised that the aircraft was becoming an invaluable tool in the arsenal of war.

The naval air arms of most countries during the First World War have, in the most, been ignored. At the onset of the war they were regarded as a fad by the military hierarchies, not worthy of serious consideration, but by the end of the war the naval air services had played their part and become serious players in the world of aviation.

Definition of 'Kills', 'Tallies' and 'Scores'

The method of scoring the totals of hostile aircraft destroyed during the First World War, used by the British, French and German air services, gave an interesting insight into human nature.

The British (including the Australians, Canadians and South Africans) would only accept the 'kill' if it could be confirmed by either a second pilot or by some other satisfactory evidence. As the British almost always fought on the enemy's side of the line, confirmation of a kill was all the more difficult.

The French command was even stricter; they would only accept confirmation of a victory when the remains of the enemy aircraft could actually be recovered. This obviously was one of the main reasons why the French pilots tried to engage the enemy over their territory.

The Germans, on the other hand, claimed victories almost at the drop of the hat. An aircraft going into a spin to carry out a manoeuvre during a fight would be often be claimed as having been shot down. Even an aircraft that had been damaged and was in the process of crashing would be claimed as a kill by all those who either dived after or had shot at it during a fight. It has to be remembered that almost all the aerial fighting took place over German-held territory. There is strong evidence that so-called 'top aces' would claim a kill, even when the aircraft had already been mortally wounded by another aircraft, by putting a burst of machine gunfire into it as it spun out of control. Some historians say that if Manfred von Richthofen's, and indeed the other German aces' scores had been subjected to the same rules as the Allies, their 'kill' counts would have been halved.

Sopwith Pusher of the Greek Navy taking off on a reconnaissance flight.

Glossary

Aeroplane   Heavier-than-air powered craft.

Airship   Lighter-than-air powered craft.

Amphibian   A seaplane fitted with wheels and floats to permit landing on either land or water.

Floatplane   An aeroplane with floats as its undercarriage, specifically designed to only land and take-off from water.

Flying boat   An aeroplane where the fuselage has a boat-shaped hull for ease of landing and taking-off from water.

Non-rigid airship An airship where the gasbags form the external shape when inflated.

Rigid airship   An airship where the gasbags are housed within a pre-designed skeletal framework.

Seaplane   Covers both flying boats and floatplanes.

Zeppelin   Rigid airship designed and built by the Zeppelin Co.

RNAS Isle of Grain from the air.

1
Royal Naval Air Service

The Royal Navy's interest in the use of aircraft on ships started, not with anything that happened in Britain, but in Virginia, USA. On Monday 14 November 1910 a man by the name of Eugene Ely roared down a wooden ramp on board the American light cruiser USS *Birmingham* in a Curtiss pusher biplane, swooped down toward the sea then upward into the sky and into history. The first time an aircraft had flown from a ship. The Americans continued to carry out experiments with ships and aircraft and all the time Britain watched with increasing interest.

In Britain the first real interest in aviation, so far as the navy was concerned, started at the Balloon Factory, Farnborough, where the first British airship was built for the army. The airship called *Nulli Secundus,* British Airship No.1, had flown over London on 5 October 1907 and around the War Office in Whitehall, creating quite a stir. The Admiralty saw the potential of such a craft, as they monitored the unrest in Europe and the rapid development of the German Zeppelins. They approached the shipbuilders Vickers, Son & Maxim, who had been building ships for the navy for a number of years, with a proposal for an airship. No one seemed to consider the fact that the company had never built anything remotely like an airship before, but nevertheless they were given the contract. The contract for 35,000 was awarded to Vickers in 1909 and work began on the construction of Naval Airship No.1, the *Mayfly*. Two years later on 22 May 1911, the *Mayfly* emerged from its building shed at Barrow-in-Furness, 512ft long and 48ft in diameter and immediately had to ride out a gale whilst tied to her mooring mast. There were misgivings about the robustness of the airship from day one and it was not until 22 September 1911 that the navy was forced to accept it. Three days later, whilst in the process of backing the *Mayfly* out of her shed, she was caught by a gust of wind and damaged beyond repair.

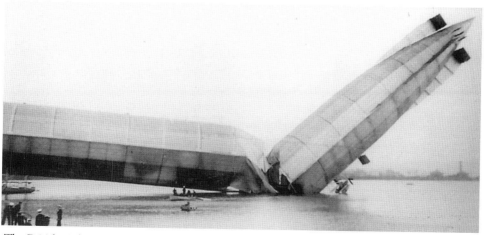

The British airship, Mayfly*, lies with her back broken after an accident whilst being removed from her floating shed at Cavendish Dock, 24 September 1911.*

The first flight from a British warship. Cdr Charles Rumney Samson about to take off from HMS Africa *in a Short on 27 January 1912.*

The navy decided that they would shift their attention to aircraft and three officers from the Royal Navy and one from the Royal Marines were sent to Eastchurch to be trained as pilots. The school was owned and run by Frank McLean, an early aviation pioneer who had several Short biplanes. Among the four pilots was a Lt C.R. Samson, RN, who was to become one of the most influential pilots in the Royal Navy. Samson was also a close friend of Winston Churchill, the First Lord of the Admiralty. He persuaded Churchill to have a flight and in 1912 he took to the air in a Short S.27 flown by Sqn Cdr A.V. Longmore. Churchill was hooked and became an ardent supporter of naval aviation. This interest later culminated in him taking flying instruction and becoming a pilot himself. More trials were carried out with a variety of different aircraft, predominantly seaplanes, as this appeared to be the most natural progression of the aeroplane as far as the navy was concerned. In December 1911, however, Lt C.R. Samson took off from the deck of the cruiser HMS *Africa,* in an S.27 No.38, and recorded a milestone in aviation history. With the success of this flight came a series of others, including the landing and take-off from the deck of HMS *Hibernia* in Weymouth Bay. To aid the progress of naval aviation, a seaplane station was set up on the Isle of Grain where trials and experiments were carried out. Three months later another station was opened up at Calshot, near Southampton, this time for operational purposes, closely followed by stations at Yarmouth, Felixstowe, Cromarty and Dundee. The war clouds had begun to gather in Europe, the Germans and the Austro-Hungarians as the main protagonists. The Royal Navy, although possessing the largest and most powerful fleet of warships in the world, realised that the aircraft had its place in any forthcoming conflict as an observation platform. On 1 July 1914 the Royal Naval Air Service (RNAS) was officially formed from the Naval Wing of the Royal Flying Corps.

When, at 2300 hours on 4 August 1914, the message, 'Commence hostilities against Germany', was flashed from the wireless room of the Admiralty to all the ships of the Royal Navy, it was accepted, as far as the Royal Navy was concerned, that their part in the war would be a struggle against the German High Seas Fleet. Both fleets had extremely powerful ships at their disposal, and the location of these ships was of paramount importance to the respective

A Short S.38 being hoisted aboard HMS Hibernia *in Weymouth Harbour.*

A Short S.38 aboard HMS Hibernia *in Weymouth Harbour being prepared for launching trials.*

HMS Hibernia *in Weymouth Bay, Dorset, in May 1912, during experimental aircraft launching trials. The aircraft on the left of the picture is a Short S.38. and the one of the right is the Short S.41.*

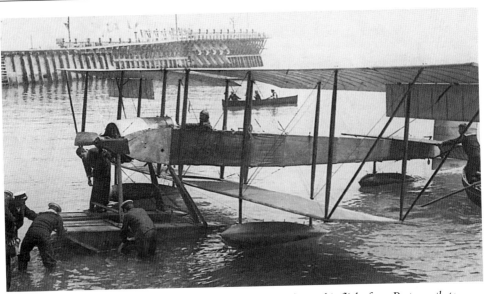

Cdr Samson in his Short S.41 at Dover on 13 July 1912, during his flight from Portsmouth to Harwich.

Naval High Commands. The Royal Navy had been building their aviation section gradually over the years and immediately their use became apparent – as the eyes and ears of the fleet. The Imperial German Navy on the other hand had been using the Zeppelin for reconnaissance, but this type of aircraft was deemed by the Royal Navy to be too slow and easily spotted.

One of the pioneers of aviation, Claude Graham-White, offered his services at the outbreak of war and was accepted and given the rank of Squadron Commander. The aerodrome at Hendon became an RNAS station and officers were sent to either Hendon, Brooklands or Bristol for their initial training before going to Eastchurch for their advanced instruction, ending in a seaplane course at Calshot near Southampton.

The first action between the two warring factions was the result of an incident off the east coast of Africa on 29 September 1914, when the German light cruiser *Königsberg* surprised the British cruiser HMS *Pegasus* cleaning out her boilers off the coast of Zanzibar and sank her. The *Königsberg* was chased by HMS *Chatham* and immediately took refuge in the delta of the Rufigi River, Tanganyika (now known as Tanzania). The Rufigi River ran for 100 miles in a plethora of channels, surrounded by mangrove swamps and impenetrable jungle, and any charts that were available were virtually useless because of the changing mud banks and sand bars. HMS *Chatham* was in a no-win situation, she could not follow the *Königsberg* into the delta and up the river, and she could not leave the mouth of the delta for fear of the light cruiser slipping out into the Indian Ocean and menacing the shipping there.

To try and approach the *Königsberg* from the land was out of the question, not only was the whole area under German control, there were no maps available and the terrain was extremely hostile. The only way to find out exactly where the German ship lay was by aerial reconnaissance. In Durban, South Africa, there was a civilian pilot by the name of H.D. Cutler giving exhibition flights in a beaten-up old 90hp Curtiss flying boat. Cutler was 'persuaded' to join the Royal Navy on a temporary basis and given the rank of Flight Sub-Lieutenant in the RNAS. The aircraft and its pilot were shipped aboard a Union-Castle liner, the *Kinfauns*

Curtiss Model F flying boat owned by Cutler at Simons Bay in November 1914. The aircraft was later requisitioned by the Admiralty for use in locating the Köniġsberg.

Castle, and taken to Niororo Island. After some repairs to the aircraft and its engine, Cutler climbed aboard and took the aircraft into the ai r. It soon became obvious that as the aircraft struggled into the air, the earlier suggestion of taking aboard an observer was out of the question. At 0700 hours on 22 November 1914, the battered flying boat struggled into the air and started out in search of the *Königsberg*. Cutler recorded the following entry in his log:

> *I headed for the mainland but ran into a heavy rainstorm and low cloud coming down to 450ft. I found myself over the land but could find no trace of the Rufigi. Having no compass I had reached the land several miles to the south of the Delta, though I was under the impression that I was north of it. I flew several miles in each direction and then turned inland but could find nothing by which I could locate my position, so as petrol was running short I turned out to sea.*

HMS Newbridge *after being sunk in the Rufigi channel as a blockade ship.*

The König*sberg, after being spotted from the air when hiding from the Royal Navy up the Rufigi River.*

Cutler put the aircraft down on the sea close to an island and was later rescued, remarkably, by the *Kinfauns Castle*, which had been told of his demise by the crew of an Arab dhow who had seen the aircraft land near the island. The following day Cutler took off on another attempt to find the cruiser *Königsberg* and this time he found her. She was moored alongside the bank twelve miles up the river. Cutler immediately radioed the information back to HMS *Chatham*, which in turn relayed it to the Admiralty. The information was later rejected on the grounds that it was impossible to get a ship of the size of the *Königsberg* that far up the river, as Admiralty charts showed the river was only navigable for the first four miles. But fate was to take a hand, as far as Cutler was concerned. As he turned the aircraft away from the German cruiser, the aircraft's engine failed and Cutler had to put the aircraft down on the river. Withering fire from the cruiser caused the aircraft to become inoperable and Cutler was captured by a raiding party from the German cruiser. He was to be a prisoner-of-war in East Africa until November 1917 – possibly the shortest career ever in the Royal Navy.

With the loss of the aircraft, the Navy realised that they were in a stalemate situation. The *Chatham* had been joined by HMS *Fox*, *Kinfauns Castle* and two armed tugs at the mouth of the river, and the *Königsberg* had no intention of leaving the comparative safety of the river whilst the Royal Navy waited for her outside. The Admiralty in London, now believing that the *Königsberg* was in fact moored up the river, decided that quickest way to dispose of this situation was to attack the *Königsberg* from the air with bombs. With this in mind, Flt Lts T.J. Cull and H.E. Watkins, were ordered to carry out the mission and were given two Type 807 Sopwith Seaplanes and a ground crew of eighteen ratings to accomplish it. The special unit was put aboard the steamer SS *Persia* at Tilbury Docks at then set sail for Zanzibar.

Almost immediately the aircraft proved to be totally unsuitable for the tropical climate and the Admiralty ordered them to be replaced with three Shorts aircraft, the Type 827. Cull accepted the replacements with grave misgivings, as he deemed them to be not a whole lot better than the Sopwiths. The aircraft arrived at Niororo Island on 23 April and, two days later, the aircraft, with Lt Cull at the controls and Leading Air Mechanic Boggis as observer, took off to try and locate the *Königsberg*. Within hours the German light cruiser had been located, and according to Cull, was in pristine condition with smoke coming from her funnels. Cull had taken with him his German 7X5 Goetz Anschutz camera, as there was no official camera available. As Cull brazenly flew alongside the ship taking photographs, the Germans opened fire and a rifle bullet struck the aircraft's oil line, forcing it to withdraw and head back for the safety of its 'mother ship'.

The hot and humid climate wreaked havoc on the aircraft. The fabric rotted, the glue started to melt and the wooden spars started to warp, in short there was a genuine worry that the aircraft could come apart in the air. Even the engines were beginning to suffer and after each flight they had to be stripped down and cleaned. It was realised that an attack from the air, using the Short Type 827, was out of the question. So it was decided to attack the *Königsberg* using two shallow draft warships that had been initially ordered from British ship-builders for the Brazilian Navy, but commandeered by the Royal Navy at the outbreak of the war, they were HMS *Severn* and *Mersey*. These two warships were ideally suited for the mission, as they had been designed for river work and had a draught of only 5ft 8in. While the two ships were making their way to the Rufigi Delta, the navy captured Mafia Island, which was situated just outside the Delta. This enabled an airstrip to be built using local labour, and on 18 June the armed liner HMS *Laurentic* arrived with four aircraft aboard, two Henry Farmans and two Caudron G.IIIs, together with their pilots and observers and ground crews.

The aircraft were unloaded and assembled and after tests, in which two of the four aircraft were badly damaged to the point of being unusable, were readied for the attack on the *Königsberg*. The two monitor warships HMS *Severn* and *Mersey* arrived on 5 July 1914 with the attack scheduled for 6 July. The aircraft radios were tuned with those of the *Severn*, *Mersey* and the flagship *Weymouth*, with Vice Admiral King-Hall aboard, which had arrived to take overall command. By this time the *Königsberg* had attracted a small fleet of British warships,

Flt Lt J.T. Cull, pilot of the aircraft that spotted for the guns that destroyed the Königsberg.

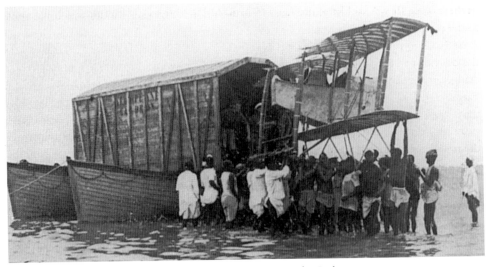

The unpacking of one of the Caudron G.III aircraft at the Rufigi Delta.

who were intent on preventing her leaving. Beside the warships already mentioned, there were three other cruisers, HMS *Pyramus, Hyacinth* and *Pioneer*, who were patrolling off shore ready to bombard the shore line as a diversionary tactic if required. At 0400 hours on the morning of 6 July, the two monitor warships slipped their anchors and made their way up the river. But German ground forces under the command of the *Königsberg's* captain, Korvettenkapitän Schoenfeld, strategically placed on the river banks, had heard the clanking of machinery and warned the small artillery crews. They opened fire as the ships passed but no damage was caused to the two monitors and they were soon out of range of the shore guns. In the meantime, Flt Lt Cull and his observer had taken off from Mafia Island and from 6,000ft, dropped two bombs on the *Königsberg*. They were seen to explode close to the ship, but caused no damage.

The Battle of Rufigi Delta had begun at 0700 hours, the *Königsberg* opened fire with four of her 105mm guns with unerring accuracy. Both the British monitors were straddled with gunfire and for the next hour the ships continued to pound each other, the Germans getting the better of the engagement. The *Severn* was taking the worst of the action and the captain decided to move her position. As he did so he noticed four German sailors high in the trees, obviously spotting on the two British ships positions for the German cruiser and relaying the information back. A well-aimed shot dispatched the four men and their position in no uncertain manner and put paid to the accuracy of the German cruiser's guns. At the end of the day, the *Severn* and the *Mersey* had fired nearly 650 rounds and the two aircraft had spent 15 hours and 19 minutes in the air between them.

The following day Vice Admiral King-Hall decided on another attack, but bad weather closed in around the small fleet and delayed matters until 11 July. At 1100 hours the *Severn* and *Mersey* moved further upstream, the *Severn* was to then anchor, while the *Mersey* proceeded a further 6,000 yards to engage the *Königsberg*. As they did so, the *Mersey* was hit by two shells from a field gun, causing some casualties. The German cruiser opened fire at 1212 hours, the first four salvoes blasting over the top of HMS *Mersey*. Minutes later a fifth salvo straddled the *Severn*, it was obvious that the Germans had a spotter relaying the positions of the targets. (It was said later, that the Germans had an officer sat in a tub which was sunk in the mud just thirty yards from where the Severn was anchored.)

At 1242 hours, with reports coming in from Sub-Lt Arnold in the Farman spotter plane, the *Severn* opened fire from 10,000 yards with her 4.7in guns. Hits were recorded on the bridge area causing considerable damage and wounding the captain, but to a cost. As the Farman circled overhead, it too was hit and forced to make an emergency landing near the *Mersey*. Both members of the crew were picked up safely. The *Severn* continued to pound away at the *Königsberg*, every salvo now scoring direct hits, until suddenly all return fire from the now stricken German cruiser ceased. Both the British monitors were withdrawn from the action and the remaining aircraft, the Caudron G.III, returned to Mafia Island, where in his excitement to let everyone know the news, the pilot overshot the landing, writing the aircraft off. This left the fleet with no aircraft to carry out a reconnaissance flight over the *Königsberg*. The RNAS had four aircraft when the action had started, now they had none, but reports came back from shore parties saying that the German cruiser was now a wreck and the crew were unloading all recoverable stores and supplies onto a lighter which had been drawn alongside. The breech blocks from the big guns were thrown overboard. Later, in a remarkable feat of endurance, the breech blocks were recovered from the river bed, the guns removed from the cruiser and manhandled overland to Dar-es-Salaam where they were in action right up until the end of the war. The Battle of the Rufigi Delta was over and one German cruiser was destroyed, but in doing so, it had been necessary to tie up seven British warships for a period of two months and lose four aircraft, but the aircraft had proved its worth. There is no doubt that without the support of the aircraft, the siege would possibly have tied up a number of British warships for the remainder of the war.

German sailors from the cruiser Königsberg *on lookout during the battle.*

*The Königsberg
steams up the
Rufigi River in an
effort to escape
from the British.*

HMS Mersey *passing across the bows of HMS* Severn *in the Rufigi River.*

HMS Severn
*in the fore-
ground with
HMS
Hyacinth
behind.*

HMS Severn *alongside the Cunard liner* Laconia, *just prior to the* Severn *leaving to engage the* Königsberg.

Henry Farman F.27. This aircraft was flown by Flt Sub-Lt H.I. Arnold during the Königsberg *incident.*

HMS Severn *towing a seaplane up the Rufigi River during the* Königsberg *incident.*

HMS Chatham *firing her guns at the* Königsberg *in the Rufigi Delta.*

A port side shot of the König sberg *wreck.*

The battered wreck of the König sberg *after her guns had been removed.*

An aerial shot of the wrecked König̈sberg.

The shell-battered König̈sberg *in the Rufigi River after the British had finished pounding her into submission.*

Some of the ten 10.5cm guns from the Königsberg *being manhandled through the jungle after the cruiser had been battered into a wreck.*

One of the 10.5cm guns from the Königsberg *at Dar-es-Salaam during the First World War.*

Winston Churchill, First Lord of the Admiralty, strides purposefully from his office in Whitehall.

Winston Churchill after his first flight in an aircraft, flown by A.V. Longmore.

Overhead shot of Cdr Samson's Sopwith Camel on board the lighter prior to the trials.

Sopwith 2F1 Camel taking off from the converted Great Eastern steamer Stockholm, *flown by Flt Lt Tomlinson.*

Flt Sub-Lts Savory and Dickinson with their B.E.2c that carried out the bombing raid on Constantinople.

Sopwith 2F1 Camel N.6623 belonging to Cdr Samson on the lighter prior to the first trials of an aircraft taking off from a lighter at sea.

2
War Clouds Gather Over Europe

Although the earlier problems with the *Mayfly* airship had dampened the enthusiasm of many of the navy's aviation supporters, the development of HMA (His Majesty's Airship) No.3 still retained some of their interest. HMA No.3 was an Astra-Torres non-rigid airship designed in 1911 by the Spanish designer Torres Quevedo, and after some small modifications carried out a series of acceptance trials for the navy. On acceptance, she joined the German-designed Parseval airship, HMA No.4, at Royal Naval Air Station Kingsnorth, and made her first flight escorting troopships that were taking the BEF (British Expeditionary Force) to France. These first flights were very successful and three more Astra-Torres airships were ordered and given the designations of HMA Nos 8, 10 and 16 respectively. As the success of the airships as escort and reconnaissance gatherers increased, thoughts turned to using the airships for a variety of other roles.

In England, in September 1914, the first wing of the RNAS was formed at Eastchurch, under the command of Wg Cdr Charles Rumney Samson, RN, and almost immediately a squadron from the wing was posted to Ostend. The squadron was to operate patrol flights along the English Channel, in order to protect the BEF from attack by Zeppelins. They were to replace the RNAS airships *Astra-Torres* and *Parseval*, that had been patrolling the Channel for some months previously. The squadron, No.1 RNAS, was equipped with the latest aircraft, the Sopwith Tabloid, which had been built by Sopwith and designed by Harry Hawker and was one of the finest aircraft of its day. Before the war, a similar version had won the Schneider Trophy at Monaco and a two-seat version had stunned crowds at the Hendon Air Display with its speed of 90mph and rate of climb of 1,200ft per minute. Physically a small aircraft, with a wing span of 25ft 6in, the Forces immediately saw the possibilities in such an aircraft and ordered a military version. It was powered by 100hp Gnome Monosoupape, had a maximum speed of a 92mph, an endurance of 3 hours and could carry two 20lb bombs.

Avro 504s about to take off to raid the Zeppelin sheds at Friedrichshafen on 21 November 1914.

Officers and men who were concerned in the attack on Friedrichshafen. The two officers seated in the middle are Flt Cdr Babbington and Sqn Cdr Featherstone-Briggs. Featherstone-Briggs was shot down during the attack and was captured.

The aircraft were soon in action and on 22 September 1914 they carried out an attack on the Zeppelin sheds at Düsseldorf – the first British air raid on Germany. The raid was a complete disaster from a military standpoint and in terms of inflicting damage. Of the four aircraft that took part, only one managed to find the target and the two bombs that were dropped failed to explode. But it did prove one thing to the Germans, they were vulnerable to attack from the air and that their homeland too could experience the ravages of war.

The RNAS established its first forward base at Antwerp in November 1914, quickly followed by a second at Belfort, France. The same month two aircraft from the base at Antwerp again attacked the Zeppelin sheds at Düsseldorf and Cologne. The two pilots, Sqn Cdr Spenser-Grey and Flt Lt R.G.L. Marix, each selected the targets, Spenser-Grey – Cologne, Marix – Düsseldorf. Spenser-Grey's target was shrouded in clouds, so he attacked a nearby railway station with limited success, but Marix found his sheds easily and dropped his two 20lb bombs from a height of 600ft. Seconds later the Zeppelin hangar erupted in an enormous fireball that reached a height of over 500ft. The two bombs had scored a direct hit not only on the hangar, but on the brand-new Zeppelin Z9 inside which had only just been completed. After coming under heavy machine-gun fire, from which his aircraft sustained considerable damage, Marix managed to coax the aircraft back to the Allied lines. Both pilots were awarded the DSO (Distinguished Service Order) for their bravery.

Four Avro 504 biplanes, Nos. 179, 873, 874 and 875, were equipped to carry four 20lb bombs and on 20 November 1914 they took off from the *Belfort*. By the time that all but one of the four aircraft had returned, they had flown 250 miles over enemy-held territory, over mountainous ranges and through extremely difficult weather conditions and bombed the Zeppelin factory at Friedrichshafen. The raid caused a great deal of damage in both material and morale to the enemy, including almost destroying the Zeppelin Z7, which was in for repairs. The one aircraft that did not return was that of Sqn Cdr Featherstone-Briggs, who was shot down by heavy machine-gun fire from the ground and was taken prisoner.

But the German army pushed relentlessly on and soon the RNAS found themselves being pushed back to Dunkirk, where they established a base. The bases they relinquished were taken over by the rapidly expanding German Naval Air Service, which established its first base at Zeebrugge.

A Royal Naval Division defending Antwerp in early October 1914 was supported by a rapidly formed balloon section. Before the balloon itself could be dispatched, the city had fallen and the section disbanded. Rear Admiral Hood, who was commanding a naval force that was supporting the Allied forces in France and Belgium, decided that the balloon could be used to help spot gunfire for his warships. The Naval Balloon section was quickly reformed and supplied with old Boer War balloons, but it was quickly discovered that the balloons were unstable and not in the best of condition. Communications between the balloon and the ground was primitive to say the least. The German kite balloon was obviously superior and a similar craft was adopted by the British who then set up a balloon depot and training course.

Then at the end of 1914 all control of the airships passed to the Royal Navy, who immediately set about ordering the building of one to their own specifications – the Sea Scout (SS). The first of these, SS-1, built in February 1915, consisted of suspending the fuselage of a

The armourers of No.214 Squadron RNAS arm bombs prior to a raid. Note the crude manufacture of the bombs with the stabilising fins riveted onto the bomb casing.

Officers of No.3 Wing RNAS. Sqn Cdr R. Bell-Davies, VC, is seated on the right.

B.E.2c beneath a Willows No.2 airship and a number of successful trials were carried out. The SS-1 was destroyed on 7 May 1915 when it collided with some telegraph wires near Dover during a training flight. The SS airship was a resounding success and over fifty were built, some being sold to foreign governments, but it had limitations. What was required was an airship that could carry out patrols in the channel for lengthy periods of time. From these requirements came the Coastal class of airship.

As with the Sea Scout, also known as the Submarine Scout, airship the fuselage of an aircraft, in this case the Avro 510, was slung beneath the envelope of one of the balloons. The undercarriage was replaced with large skids that stretched the length of the fuselage and horizontal stabilisers and elevators were fitted to the bottom lobes of the airship's envelope. Carrying a crew of four, the Coastal airship could carry bombs and a wireless operator, and was armed with two Lewis machine guns for self-protection. A total of ten Coastal class airships were built and all served with distinction. Over the next few years a large number of different classes of airship were built, the Coastal Star, SSZ, SSP, SSE and SSTs, making Britain one of the foremost users of the airship in the world – culminating in the building of the large rigid airships, the R-class.

Although the war centred in Europe and Middle East, it also touched other countries such as Ireland. In October 1914 it was discovered that a minefield had been laid by a German ship off the coast of Donegal near Tory Island. It took almost a year to find the extent of the field and to 'sweep' it clean. U-boats were often seen in the Irish Sea and in February 1915, three steamers were sunk off the Mersey. These activities showed that the U-boats were slowly gaining control of the seas around Ireland and could easily intercept merchant ships approaching from the Atlantic carrying ammunition and necessary war supplies. This was highlighted on 7 May 1915, when the passenger liner RMS *Lusitania* was torpedoed by the German submarine U-20, commanded by Kapitänleutnant Walter Schweiger, with the loss of 1,198 men and women. A surface fleet was quickly assembled in an attempt to patrol these waters, but it wasn't until the arrival of the airships of the RNAS in 1916 that the battle against the U-boat threat began to have an effect. It soon became obvious, such were the losses of merchant ships, that if the battle against the U-boats wasn't quickly won, Britain would be in dire straits. Patrol stations were set up in Ireland at Ballyliffin, Co. Donegal; Johnstown Castle, Co. Wexford; Larne, Co. Antrim and Malahide Castle, Co. Dublin. The use of the airship for long periods over the expanses of water proved to be ideal, as the airship could hover over given points but only as long as the weather held. The airship was susceptible to a variety of problems such strong thermal currents that were common in the areas around the coast of Ireland and sudden temperature changes bringing with them rapid changes of weather. The types of airship used were the SS, SSZ, Coastal, Coastal Star, and North Sea Types, all of which were eminently suitable. Slowly the U-boat threat lessened and the arrival of American submarines and flying boats in Ireland, hastened the demise of the U-boat around Ireland and in the Irish Sea. Between May 1915 and September 1916 four additional balloon ships were converted from merchantmen, *City of Oxford*, *Canning*, *Menelaeus* and *Hector,* and by the end of the war more than 152 vessels had the facility of carrying and using observation balloons – no other navy employed balloons on such a large scale.

The war in Gallipoli was not going at all well. It had been hoped that defeating the Turkish Army would force the Germans and Austrians to rush reinforcements to the area and so relieve the pressure on the Western Front and the Caucasus. But the Turkish troops had proved to be more resilient than had been anticipated, and the naval bombardment of the shoreline had had little or no effect on the Turkish guns, mainly because they had no idea

RMS Lusitania.

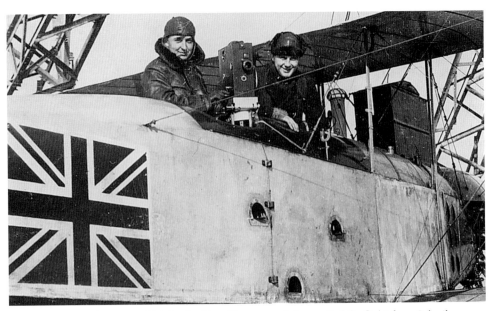

Eastchurch-built Short Type 830 fitted with a film camera being readied for flight from Salonika.

where they were placed. It was decided to use balloons as observation posts to report on the build up of enemy forces and to spot for the naval gunfire.

The Admiralty acquired a tramp steamer at the beginning of March 1915, the SS *Manica*, and fitted her out as a balloon ship in just seventeen days. A sloping deck from the waist to the forecastle was fitted, a hydrogen compressor installed, a winch that was connected to the main engines, a wireless telegraphy hut and living quarters for the officers and men, together with a French balloon. On 9 April the ship arrived in the Aegean and started its assignment The information supplied proved to be most valuable during troop landings and the naval gunfire bombardment of the defences.

Information coming back from the Aegean about the use of the *Manica*'s observation balloon, prompted the Admiralty to consider the use of a similar ship with the Grand Fleet. A report from Sqn Cdr J.D. Mackworth, who was in charge of *Manica*'s balloon section, suggested that the success of the project in the Aegean would warrant consideration in the building of properly designed kite balloon ships.

Tests were carried out using the seaplane carrier *Engadine* under the personal supervision of Rear Admiral Hood. In a letter to Admiral Beatty, Hood said:

> *I think I have proved the value of the kite balloon for reconnaissance purposes; in a suitable vessel the strategic and tactical value will be very great; at 3,000 feet there will be a radius of vision of 60 miles and the communication will not be the sketchy kind in use from an aeroplane, but will be conversation by telephone from a skilled observer sitting comfortably in a basket, to a responsible officer in the balloon ship, who with efficient W/T and all signal books and codes at hand, will rapidly signal by the most efficient method the information…*

This letter, together with the letter from Sqn Cdr Mackworth, gave Admiral Beatty the idea of replacing some of the seaplanes on the *Campania* (the ex-Cunard liner) with a kite balloon.

Admiral Jellicoe then joined in asking if he too could have a balloon ship, but the Board of the Admiralty at that time seemed, as usual, to be out of touch with reality and were still living in the past. They refused the recommendation saying that the building of such a vessel would be costly and lengthy in time, and that fast merchant ships for other war purposes were more of a priority. The *Campania,* however, during its second refit was adapted to operate a balloon, which was all that Admiral Beatty had ever asked for.

One criticism of the use of the balloon, however, did have some merit. If the balloons were to be used by the Grand Fleet for observation purposes, at the proposed height of 3,000ft, it could also give away the position of the Fleet to the enemy. It was decided that observation balloons could operate from battleships, battlecruisers, light cruisers and some destroyers so winches and facilities were installed. This did not necessarily mean that they all would carry balloons, merely that they would have the capacity to do so. The utility of the balloon was highlighted during the anti-submarine campaign of 1917 when the destroyer HMS *Patriot* spotted the German submarine U-69 commanded by Kapitänleutnant Wilhelms at a distance of twenty-eight miles. She subsequently carried out a depth charge attack and sank the U-boat off the Shetland Islands. It is a fact that convoys protected by destroyers carrying observation balloons suffered fewer losses.

Vice Admiral Sir Sackville H. Carden, who was commanding a naval squadron off the Dardanelles in an effort to intercept the German battleships *Goeben* and *Breslau,* was asked to head a naval expedition that was to carry out a bombardment of the Dardanelles. When asked to estimate the type and number of ships he would require for such an engagement, he replied that amongst the obvious heavy-gunned ships, he would require four seaplanes and the seaplane carrier *Foudre.* The need for frequent observation and gun spotting flights would be imperative and the *Foudre* was the only vessel in the Mediterranean capable of repairing and maintaining the aircraft.

One of the very rare lighter moments with No.1 Wing RNAS with their very 'secret experimental' aircraft, Dunkirk 1915. The British naval officer, third from left, is Flt Lt S. V. Sippe, who took part in the raid on the Zeppelin sheds at Freidrichshafen.

During one incident, after the German battlecruiser *Goeben* had attacked *Imbros*, Royal Naval Flt Sub-Lt Robert W. Peel attempted to bomb the battlecruiser. During the attempt his aircraft came under attack from German aircraft and he was only saved by the interception of a Greek naval fighter aircraft flown by Capt. Aristides C. Moraitinis. Peel said that it was only the superb flying of Moraitinis that drove the German attackers away.

It transpired that five years earlier, Moraitinis, together with his observer in their Maurice Farman floatplane, had been actively involved in carrying out reconnaissance missions against Turkish warships in the Dardanelles. In one of the missions, they attempted to drop handmade bombs (probably converted hand grenades) on the Turkish Fleet. Although the attacks were unsuccessful, this made them the first serving naval aviators in the world to carry out an operational combat mission against an enemy.

A postscript to the *Goeben's* attack on *Imbros* – after the attack the battlecruiser became grounded in the Dardanelles on 20 January 1918. Whilst the Germans struggled to get the ship off, the British carried out as series of bombing raids and subjected the *Goeben* to over 200 attacks and a total of 180 bombs (15 tons) were dropped. Such was their inaccuracy that only two of the bombs actually struck the ship, causing minor damage. The end result was that the ship's refloating was delayed for an additional two days.

Problems for the RNAS arose when the Admiralty ordered the base at Port Said to send six of its eight seaplanes to join up with Vice Admiral Sackville's force. But two of the seaplanes had already been lost, three were aboard the seaplane carrier *Annes*, which was with the naval force in the Gulf of Smyrna, the remaining two were aboard the *Raven II* off the coast of Palestine and that left only one at Port Said.

The problem was solved by activating the aircraft carrier *Ark Royal* which had undergone a radical re-design and was now ready for sea. Originally designed as a tramp steamer, the

HMS Engadine *hoisting a Short 184 aboard for servicing.*

Sopwith 2F1 Camel from HMS Calliope *being transported back to the ship after a successful take off.*

Ark Royal was built with a hangar below deck to which access was gained by a large sliding hatch fitted flush to the deck. She also had two steam cranes mounted either side of the deck to handle seaplanes. She sailed for the Aegean on 1 February 1915 with a complement of six seaplanes, three Sopwith 807s; a Short Admiralty 136, the most rugged and dependable of all the machines, and two Wight Type A1 Improved Navy-planes.

Arriving off the Greek island of Tenedos on 17 February, the *Ark Royal* prepared for the bombardment of Gallipoli which began two days later.

The intention was to use the aircraft from the *Ark Royal* to spot for the naval guns, but the sea conditions were such, that during the month of February only a couple of flights were able to get off the water. Coupled with engine problems that most of the aircraft suffered (the Short 136, the most reliable of all the aircraft, suffered sixteen engine failures out of twenty-six flights between 17 February and 31 May 1915), they also had to contend with the unre-liability of air-to-surface communications. The use of aircraft under these conditions was becoming farcical. To be fair the wireless sets used had been built by the Sterling Telephone Co. to the design of a RNAS officer and were still in the development stage and really should not have been put to the test under battle conditions.

But necessity is the mother of invention, and the aerial observers and the gunnery officers developed their own system of signals and codes to overcome the problems with the W/T and it started to work. Unfortunately the only guns that were spotted were relatively minor ones; the large mobile howitzers which caused most of the damage remained unscathed.

The debacle continued and by 18 March 1915, the British battleships HMS *Irresistible* and *Ocean* had been sunk and the *Inflexible* had been severely damaged. The French had also lost the *Gaulois* and the *Suffren* – they were sunk by a line of mines that had been laid parallel to the shoreline by the Turkish minelayer *Nousret*. These mines should have been spotted by the aircraft from the *Ark Royal*, but never were. The blame for this debacle was laid at the door of the RNAS as the aircraft from the *Ark Royal* had failed to spot the mines during observation flights over the area which, in the opinion of the Admiralty, they should have done. It is accepted that had the aircraft been able to do the job they had been given, a great deal of damage could have been inflicted on the Turkish gun positions.

The need for aircraft reconnaissance missions and bombing raids was recognised by the Army and when they asked Lord Kitchener for the RFC to reinforce their troops, he angrily refused. The reason was probably that in reality there were none that could be spared, as all the aircraft that could were at the Front in Europe. The total air fleet in this theatre of war consisted of six seaplanes operating from the seaplane-carrier *Ark Royal* and two aircraft operating from the island of Tenedos, twenty miles to the south. They were later supported by No.3 Squadron RNAS, under the command of Cdr Charles R. Samson, who arrived on 4 March 1915 at Tenedos where an airfield had been prepared. Samson was probably one of the most experienced pilots that Britain had and he wasted no time in getting his squadron up to battle readiness. Nearly all his observers were volunteers with virtually no experience whatsoever of aerial observation. The only criteria that seems to have been required was that they were very light in weight.

25 April 1915 was the date scheduled for the Gallipoli landings, so No.3 Squadron took to the air at every opportunity between March and April to photograph and carry out reconnaissance on the beaches, bombing shore batteries and camps. When the landing started on 25 April, Cdr Samson's squadron supported those at Cale Helles, aircraft from the *Ark Royal* and *Manica* supported the ANZAC (Australian-New Zealand Army Corps) in the North. The aircraft contribution to the Gallipoli bloodbath was disappointing at first, but once the troops were ashore they carried out constant reconnaissance flights and spotted for the shore artillery. They also carried out bombing raids on gun positions, camps and troop movements. Within weeks the Turkish bombardment of the beaches had decreased markedly, emphasising the work of the reconnaissance missions and artillery spotting flights.

At the end of May 1915, the *Ark Royal* was withdrawn to help carry out diversionary operations in the eastern Mediterranean. The German U-boat U-21 took advantage of her absence and attacked and sank the British battleships *Triumph* (25 May) and *Majestic* (27 May).

Sopwith 2F1 Camel N6623 being prepared for the first attempted flight from a lighter. The pilot is Cdr Samson.

Lt Eric Breed RNAS launches off the gun platform of HMS Malaya.

The arrival of the U-21 in the Aegean was the cause of great concern as there was now no anti-submarine patrol. Such was the alarm that the majority of the Allied fleet, including the battleship *Queen Elizabeth* and the *Ark Royal*, which had a maximum speed of only 11 knots, withdrew. This left the troops on the shore with greatly reduced naval fire support. *Ark Royal* withdrew to Mudros and was replaced by the much faster seaplane carrier *Ben-my-Chree*. The Short 184 aircraft of the *Ben-my-Chree* carried out the first aerial torpedo attacks during this campaign. On 12 August 1915 a Short 184 from the seaplane carrier *Ben-my-Chree*, piloted by Flt Cdr C.H.K. Edmonds, carried out the first successful torpedo attack from the air, when he sank a 5,000ton Turkish supply vessel *Mahmut Sevket Pasa*.

The Turkish version of this attack however differs greatly from that of Cdr Edmonds inasmuch as the vessel attacked was said by the Turks to weigh 24,490 gross tons and was not sunk by the torpedo, as it failed to explode. They also said that the ship was safely towed to Constantinople. Cdr Edmonds' version seems to be the more likely one in this event, as it is unlikely that the Turkish merchant fleet of 1915 had a ship of such tonnage and, furthermore, they don't explain why it was necessary to tow their ship into port if it was not damaged.

Five days later another Short 184 from the seaplane-carrier torpedoed a large tug in False Bay. The use of the torpedo from the air had become another weapon to add to the naval aircraft's ever expanding weapon inventory.

The Gallipoli campaign dragged on into stalemate. The loss of human life was horrendous; there was also a loss of major battleships and other craft and, even after a second landing, had resulted in more horrendous casualties. The whole bloody debacle was a mixture of high level incompetence, almost non-existent planning and a neanderthal type of thinking that if you throw enough bodies into the fray, the weight alone would be enough to win through. The result was the senseless loss of 50,000 men.

*RNAS trucks take Turkish POWs to help clear the RNAS airfield after a bombing raid,
Gallipoli, 1915.*

RNAS officers receive awards from King George V during his visit to the Belgian front in 1916.

It would be fair to say that the aerial work carried out by the RNAS over Gallipoli could have equally been carried out by the RFC, but Lord Kitchener refused to allow the RFC to do the work. Fortunately for the Army, the RNAS was in the area at the time spotting for the battleships and the experienced gained in this field was an advantage that could not be disregarded.

In May 1916 Rear-Admiral Mark C.K. Kerr was given command of the British Adriatic Squadron. Admiral Kerr had obtained his pilot's licence two years earlier and was a strong advocate for the use of aircraft in the hunting of submarines. He immediately applied to the Admiralty for aircraft to build a squadron of reconnaissance craft/bombers. His request was turned down because he was told that the French and Italian navies already had aircraft in the Adriatic carrying out these duties. Kerr, not one to be phased by refusal, immediately requested a kite-balloon ship so as to provide the anti-submarine ships and drifters with an observation platform. The Admiralty acceded to his request, but not for a kite-balloon ship, but for aircraft. There appeared to be no reason for their sudden change of decision, but it is thought that information passed to them regarding submarines diving deep to avoid the anti-submarine nets gave them cause to think a balloon would not spot them. Also the French and Italian navies were having very limited success in curbing the activities of the German U-boats in the Adriatic.

A base was set up at Otranto under the command of Commodore Murray Sueter (later Rear Admiral) and four Short 827 and six 184 seaplanes sent. Sueter was not a pilot, but he was a man of vision, and had been one of those responsible for bringing the use of radio to submarines against some of the stiffest opposition in the Admiralty. He had been the first Director of the Admiralty Air Department but after the debacle of the Dardanelles, which saw Winston Churchill, the First Civil Lord of the Admiralty removed from office, he was replaced with equal speed. His removal was not that unexpected for he had been a thorn in the side of the Lords of the Admiralty for some time regarding his pursuance of an aviation arm in the navy.

RNAS Dundee.

Short 827 about to take off from the shallows in East Africa.

Murray Sueter's aim was to carry out bombing attacks on Pola, Fiume and Cattaro. Pola was where submarines were being assembled from parts sent by rail from Germany, the torpedoes were being manufactured at Fiume, and Cattaro was the main naval base. If he could cause substantial damage to the manufacturing plants there, it could reduce the casualties in the Adriatic considerably. But there were problems; the Short seaplanes carrying one torpedo and, even carrying no observer, had a very limited range. In fact, they could not fly across the Adriatic, carry out a bombing raid and return, as they could not carry enough fuel.

It was decided to tow the floatplanes on wooden rafts to within fifty miles of the targets and then float them off. The aircraft would take off and attack their respective targets and return. On 2 September 1917, a force was set up and the rafts, with their aircraft aboard, were towed to within fifty to sixty miles of their targets. Protected by light cruisers and destroyers, the aircraft were prepared for launching. Then suddenly the weather worsened until the whole force were in the teeth of a gale. The aircraft, made of plywood and fabric, were in danger of being destroyed by the large waves, so the whole mission was abandoned and the force returned to its base. This was the one and only time that an attack of this kind was attempted on bases across the Adriatic.

The arrival of six Sopwith Baby floatplanes and six Sopwith 1½ Strutters was a welcome addition and a new base was opened up at Taranto for stores and the repair and assembly of new aircraft. In June 1917 patrols with the Sopwith 1½ Strutters began and between June and September thirteen submarines were spotted and attacked with 65lb bombs but, although a number of hits were claimed and oil was seen coming to the surface, no actual sinkings were recorded. The success against the enemy submarines was not the success hoped for, but it is right to say that attacks against Allied shipping fell off dramatically during this period and this can be ascribed to the constant air patrols that made the enemy submariners think twice before attacking a convoy.

The progress gained in the Adriatic had not gone unnoticed back in London and when a letter arrived from Vice Admiral Hon. Sir Somerset Arthur Gough-Calthorpe supporting the

Sopwith Pup N6438 being readied for launch from aboard ship.

work Commodore Sueter was doing arrived at the Admiralty, it was decided to extend the operations to cover the Mediterranean. Three more seaplane-carriers, *Engadine, Riviera* and *Vindex,* were fitted out with stores and additional aircraft and they joined the two other carriers *Empress* and *Manxman.* Although the seaplane-carriers operated as floating bases, they came under the direct command of the Commander-in-Chief in Malta.

The seaplanes were now able to fly reconnaissance/bombing missions over enemy positions with much more accuracy and dependability that ever before. Slowly but surely the enemy were worn down and the control of the sea lanes in the Adriatic and the Mediterranean lay safely in the hands of the Allies.

On 9 January 1917 the seaplane carrier *Ben-my-Chree* was sunk at Castelorizo Island off the Turkish coast surprisingly enough by artillery fire from the shore. She was the only aviation ship sunk by enemy fire during the war.

A new squadron was formed at the beginning of 1916 – the East Indies and Egyptian Seaplane Squadron (EI&ESS). Initially commanded by Sqn Cdr Cecil J. L'Estrange Malone, the squadron operated in the Aegean and eastern Mediterranean from Salonika to Port Said. In May, command was passed to Sqn Cdr Samson who increased the area of operation to encompass parts of the Indian Ocean in an effort to track down the German commerce raider *Wolf.* During several operations in the Red Sea, the EI&ESS gave aerial support to the insurgent Arab tribes led by T.E. Lawrence. The rebellion against Turkish rule had started in Hejaz in June 1916 and the Arab tribes had started guerrilla operations. They were supported by seaplanes of the RNAS which carried out reconnaissance and bombing missions on the railway that ran north from Hejaz. As the war progressed the RFC took over the role of covering the insurgents and the Army from the air.

There were a number of forgotten theatres of the war in the Middle East, and one was in German East Africa. The territory, now called Tanzania, had an area of 250,000 square miles, commanded by General von Lettow-Vorbeck, who was in the unenviable position of being completely surrounded by Allied troops. Von Lettow-Vorbeck realised that there was no hope of being relieved until Germany was victorious in Europe and so concentrated on tying up as many Allied troops as he possibly could. He had no air force, but the Allies had both RFC and RNAS units in the area carrying out observation missions. At this point one would have thought that the Germans were at a distinct disadvantage, but such was the terrain, climate and the difficulty in maintaining air-to-ground communication, this was not so. Ground troops could hide very easily in the bush and jungles and the campaign waged by the Germans in this area was a very long and painful one.

The campaign in Salonika was another forgotten campaign, in some respects deliberately forgotten. It was a joint Anglo-French campaign that had initially been set up to protect Serbia but by the time the force had been mobilised Serbia had fallen to the Austrians. What the Anglo-French forces managed to do was create a bridgehead around Salonika, where more than half-a-million British, French, Italian, Greek, Albanian, Serbian and Montenegran soldiers controlled a 150-mile front consisting of an almost impenetrable mountain barrier. The Germans called the area 'the largest Allied concentration camp' because, with their backs to the sea and facing a mountain barrier, there was nowhere the Allies could go. Initially the RNAS and the RFC were formed into a composite squadron and carried out reconnaissance and photographic missions in their Sopwith 1½ Strutters and B.E.12s, but later in 1917, bombing missions became the order of the day. The Germans retaliated with bombing raids on Allied airfields, neither force achieving a great deal. At the beginning of May 1918 the German bombing squadrons were sent back to the Western Front as the Allied offensive there began to gain momentum.

Crude but effective, gunnery instruction for both pilots and observers.

RNAS crew about to set off on patrol in a French Breguet bomber. The figure to the right with his back to the camera is said to be the designer of the aircraft, M. Breguet.

A Turkish 6in shell bursting near the RNAS aerodrome on Long Island in the Gulf of Symrna in the East Mediterranean. The airfield was the home to No.2 Wing RNAS. Near the hangar can be seen a Nieuport, Henri Farman and a dummy aeroplane in the making. When the dummy aeroplane was completed it was placed in the middle of the field. The Turkish Army fired over seventy shells at it and still did not hit it.

Sopwith Baby N1064 being hoisted aboard a seaplane-carrier.

Sopwith Baby seaplane on the water with the pilot about to release a carrier pigeon.

The Riviera *hoisting a Sopwith Bay aboard.*

Short 184 flying boat being hoisted aboard the seaplane-carrier HMS Ark Royal.

Sopwith Pup N6454 being hoisted from the below deck hangar aboard HMS Furious. Note the tight fit of the deck opening.

The converted seaplane-carrier Manxman, *once an Isle of Man steamer.*

The seaplane-carrier Ben-My-Chree, *converted from an Isle of Man steamer.*

HMS Campania, *the ex-Cunard liner, after being converted to a seaplane-carrier.*

Wight Type A (Improved) being hoisted aboard the HMS Ark Royal *in the Dardanelles.*

A Sopwith Pup being readied for hoisting aboard a battleship after being floated out on a pontoon.

Loading a Short 184, N9290, on board HMS Pegasus.

Excellent overhead shot of a Sopwith 2F1 Camel on its launching platform aboard a cruiser.

Officers of No.1 Wing RNAS.

Lts Carey, Allan and Mackenzie of No.1 Wing RNAS. Carey and Mackenzie are about to take off on a reconnaissance mission.

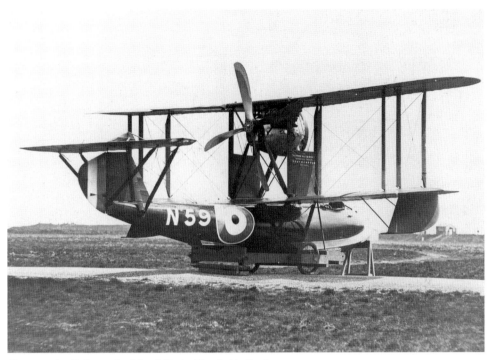

Supermarine Baby at the Isle of Grain Naval Air Station.

Lt Melvin Rattray takes off from the launching platform aboard the battleship HMS Queen Elizabeth *in his Sopwith 1½ Strutter.*

Lt S.D. Culley's Sopwith 2F1 Camel being towed on its lighter during trials in the Solent.

This Sopwith B.3878 on ditching trials looked very much like a crash. A hydrovane is fitted on its tail.

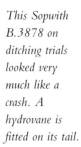

The pilot of a Sopwith 1F Camel being rescued after ditching close to the lighter after trials.

Flt Sub-Lts R. Mulock and Beard of No. 1 Wing RNAS about to take off for a bombing sortie against Zeppelin sheds at Evere, near Brussels. Each of the aircraft carried six 20lb bombs below the fuselage.

Instructor (left) and student pilot about to leave on an instruction flight in an FBA (Franco-British-Aviation) flying boat.

Lt Eric Breed about to board his aircraft on HMS Malaya.

Flt Cdr A.W. Bigsworth of No.1 Wing RNAS in front of his Avro 504b No.1009 in which he attacked and badly damaged a Zeppelin over Ostend.

3
The Birth of the Aircraft Carrier

The arrival from America of John Porte, an Englishman who had worked for the American Curtiss Co., was to herald the birth of a new seaplane – the H.4. He was commissioned into the Navy and given the rank of Squadron Commander in the RNAS. He persuaded the Admiralty to purchase two Curtiss flying boats which were evaluated at RNAS Felixstowe in November 1914. Satisfied with the results, although there were some reservations about the seaworthiness of the hull, the Admiralty ordered a further sixty-two, eight of which were to be built in England under licence and were given the designation Curtiss H.4.

Porte oversaw the development of the Curtiss H.4 and solved the problem of the hull by modifying its shape. This gave the H.4 better take-off and landing characteristics making it a much safer and stable aircraft to fly. During the next few years the Curtiss H.4 was one of the mainstay operational aircraft of the Navy and also one of the most reliable.

The airship was still being favoured by the Admiralty in London, although pressure was beginning to be applied with regard to the use of seaplanes. The airship had a longer duration than the aircraft and could be used with greater efficiency, although its manoeuvrability and ability to defend itself it left a lot to be desired. Experiments were carried out using a BE2a attached to the underside of the airship. The idea was that when the airship reached a suitable height the aircraft would be released, enabling it to carry out an extended patrol – at least that was the theory. One experiment was carried out at RNAS Kingsnorth, Kent, on 21 February 1916 by two naval officers, Lt Cdr de Courcy Ireland and Cdr Usbourne. Their aircraft was slung beneath SS airship AP1 and attached at the front and rear of the aircraft by locking devices. The airship took off carrying the aircraft and its two crew, but they let the airship get too much height before they released the aircraft. As they released the aircraft, the sudden loss of envelope pressure caused the front of the aircraft to be prematurely released. The sudden jerk threw Lt Cdr Ireland out of the aircraft to his death, and as it did so the rear locking device holding the aircraft to the airship sheared off, damaging the aircraft's controls. The result was that the aircraft plunged to the ground, killing Cdr Usbourne in turn.

The Royal Naval aircraft used in raids had, up to this point, been used primarily from land bases, although its original task was to carry out reconnaissance flights for the fleet. This role was at present being carried out by seaplanes from shore bases and it was soon realised that it had neither the range or the fuel carrying capacity to enable it to operate further than around the coasts. The alternative was fly aircraft from ships and return them to ships.

The navy had had one 'aircraft carrier', HMS *Hermes,* which was capable of carrying three seaplanes, but she had been torpedoed by a U-boat in the English Channel on 31 October. The Admiralty then turned its attention to a tramp steamer that they had purchased in 1913 whilst it was in the process of being built. It was decided to redesign the ship, moving the funnel and bridge abaft, leaving the fore part of the deck clear to take aircraft, much like modern oil tankers. She was commissioned as HMS *Ark Royal* in 1915, only for her designers to discover that the aircraft she was designed to take had become bigger and heavier. She was relegated to becoming a seaplane tender, but served with some distinction during the war. She joined three other seaplane tenders, HMS *Engadine, Riviera* and *Empress,* which had been

An experiment using a B.E.2c attached to an SS airship was carried out by Cdr Usbourne and Lt-Cdr de Courcy Ireland. This experiment went tragically wrong when the front wires holding the aircraft were suddenly and unexpectedly released while the rear wires remained holding the aircraft. The aircraft flipped over onto its back throwing Usbourne out. Then the rear wires snapped and the aircraft, with Ireland still aboard, crashed into the ground killing him. This photograph shows the B.E.2c and the SS airship just as they were lifting off to carry out the experiment.

converted from cross-channel steamers, but these 'aircraft carriers' had speeds of 21 knots, which enabled them to keep pace with the fleet.

It was these additions to the fleet, that persuaded the Admiralty to launch a seaborne attack on the German Zeppelin sheds at Nordholtz, just south of Cuxhaven. This was to be the first naval air operation to be carried out by the Royal Navy, and the first from aircraft carriers. The attack, if successful, would create deep concern into the German High Command and prove that the RNAS had a very serious role to play in the war. The Cuxhaven Raid, as it was to become known, was to do just that.

At 1700 hours on 24 December 1914, the aircraft carriers HMS *Engadine*, *Empress* and *Riviera*, escorted by two cruisers, HMS *Arethusa* and *Undaunted*, and eight destroyers, HMS *Lawford*, *Lennox*, *Leonidas*, *Lookout*, *Lydiard*, *Lysander*, *Miranda* and *Minos* which, in turn, were escorted by ten submarines, slipped out of Harwich harbour. The submarines were also to be used as rescue boats in the event of any of the aircraft having to ditch in the sea. By 0530 hours on Christmas morning, the two cruisers were on station forty nautical miles due north of the Friesian island of Wangerooge awaiting the arrival of the three aircraft carriers and their aircraft. Complete radio silence had been observed by the fleet but they had been spotted by a number of trawlers whilst crossing the channel, one of which transmitted a radio signal. One hour later a coded radio transmission from Heligoland was intercepted, which contained the German navy's known coded word for 'urgent'. The whole fleet was put on full alert, but by the time the three aircraft carriers were in position, no enemy aircraft had appeared.

On the three aircraft carriers, the crews of the aircraft had been briefed. Not only was the primary target, the Zeppelin sheds at Cuxhaven, to be attacked, but reconnaissance flights were to be carried out regarding the location of German warships and their exact positions. At 0730 hours on Christmas morning, the seven seaplanes took to the air and set a course for Cuxhaven. As they disappeared from view, the German Zeppelin L6 was spotted approaching the fleet. It dropped two bombs in the direction of HMS *Empress*, neither of which hit the ship, and rapidly moved away when the cruiser HMS *Undaunted* opened fire.

Meanwhile the seven aircraft headed for Wilhelmshaven and the German naval fleet. The observers on board frantically took down as many details as they could regarding the number of ships at anchor, identifying individual ships and which ones were already underway and heading for the open sea. Accurate heavy machine-gun fire and anti-aircraft fire filled the skies around the aircraft, causing all of them to suffer some form of damage. The Zeppelin sheds were never attacked, although a number of bombs were dropped on the German warships that were lying at anchor but causing very little damage. Realising that they were losing fuel and the aircraft were badly damaged, the seven seaplanes headed back toward their mother ships. Of the seven aircraft that took off, only two managed to get back to the aircraft carriers. The remainder had to ditch in the sea and the crews picked up by British submarines.

In terms of damage the raid was a total failure, but in terms of information on the German fleet, it was a great success. It also caused the German Naval High Command to rush troops to this and other vulnerable areas, in order to reinforce the anti-aircraft defences. This of course tied up a great number of troops and weapons for the duration of the war. A new concept of war had been introduced to the world, one which was to lay the foundations for a new type of navy and to alter forever the way naval wars were fought.

HMS Hermes *sinking in the English Channel after being torpedoed by the German submarine U-27 commanded by Kapitänleutnant Wegener.*

HMS Engadine.

The seaplane-carrier *Empress.*

The seaplane-carrier *Riviera.*

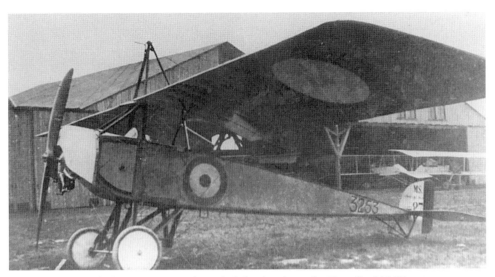

Flt Sub-Lt Warneford's Morane-Parasol in which he shot down the Zeppelin LZ.37.

The German retaliation for the raid was almost instant. At the beginning of January 1915, the Kaiser ordered the Imperial German Navy to ready three of their Zeppelins, the L3, L4 and L6 and launch an immediate attack on England. The attack, he specified, was to be on military targets, i.e. dockyards, airfields etc., but not on towns and specifically not on London. Attacks were made on the east coast of England, mostly on towns, where civilians were killed and wounded – so much for the military targets.

The RNAS endeavoured to intercept these Zeppelin raids as best they could, but they had no aircraft capable of climbing to the heights at which the majority of the Zeppelins attacked. On 7 June 1915, however, the RNAS scored its first major success, when Flt Sub-Lt 'Rex' Warneford attacked and destroyed the German Zeppelin LZ37, when it was returning from a patrol. Flying a Morane-Saulnier Type L, parasol-winged fighter, Warneford attacked the heavily armed LZ37 as it passed over Bruges, raking it with machine-gun fire from stem to stern. As the gas inside suddenly ignited, the LZ37 turned into a flaming inferno and plunged to the ground on top of a convent just outside Ghent. Remarkably, one member of the crew, Steuermann (helmsman) Alfred Mühler, survived the crash with only minor injuries, although a number of civilians were killed and injured when the burning wreckage crashed on top of them, including a nun and a number of orphan children.

The arrival from America in May 1917 of the Curtiss H.12, a much larger seaplane was a welcome addition to the RNAS's fleet of aircraft. Like the H.4, the H.12 had a problem with its hull's seaworthiness and again John Porte carried out modifications. The Navy, now satisfied that the aircraft had been accepted by the evaluation pilots, ordered seventy-one from Curtiss. The H.12 was named the 'Large America' and the H.4 'Little America'.

The H.12 could carry out operational sorties of between five and six hours, carried four gunners armed with Lewis machine guns and had a 230lb bomb mounted beneath each wing. Four seaplane anti U-boat patrols were set up in an octagonal configuration sixty miles across and covering 4,000 square miles, called the 'Spider's Web'. Their first success happened within one week of it being set up. The German U-boat UC36, commanded by Kapitänleutnant Buch, was making its way to its base at Wilmshaven when it was spotted on the surface by an

Sopwith Schneider seaplane in flight over the sea off Calshot.

H.12 'Large America' flown by Flt Sub-Lts Morrish and Boswell. The U-boat was attacked with both machine gun fire and bombs, and subsequently sunk with all hands.

The success of the Curtiss H.4s and H.12s led British designers to create the Felixstowe F2A. John Porte was again heavily involved in the design of the hull and its construction. The wings and tail came from Curtiss and was extremely sturdy. Powered by two 345hp Rolls-Royce Eagle VIII engines, the F2A could stay aloft on patrol for up to six hours on full tanks and nine hours using additional fuel carried on board in tins. It was also renowned as an extremely manoeuvrable fighting aircraft as was experienced by fourteen German seaplanes when they came across four F2As and one H.12 on a 'Spiders Web' sortie. During the fight two of the F2As were forced down with fuel line trouble, whilst the remaining two F2As and the H.12 fought the running battle with the Germans. Six of the German seaplanes were shot down with no losses or injuries to the British, the remaining eight German seaplanes departed having been well and truly beaten. The seaplane had established itself.

The use of the aeroplane from a ship at sea was fraught with danger, however, because the instruments and techniques for aerial navigation at the time were crude to say the least. This was emphasised more than once even for the most experienced pilot. One example was when Flt Cdr B.D. Kilner took off from HMS *Vindex* on 25 September 1917 chasing after a German airship, and was never seen again. The airship never reported seeing him or having any contact with any aircraft at that time. One thing that has to be remembered is that, unlike an airfield which remains static, a ship moves, and finding the ship after a mission requires a good knowledge of navigation.

By far one of the largest seaplane carrier to enter service with the RNAS was the former Cunard liner (20,000 tons) *Campania* on 1 May 1915. She had been on the Liverpool to New York sailing for a number of years and had a top speed of 21 knots enabling her to keep pace with the fleet. Initially the *Campania* was offered to the government on charter at a cost of £13,000 a month and any modifications made to be removed and the liner restored back to her original condition. The government decided that this was not practicable and the *Campania* was bought outright for the sum of £180,000. She was then sent to Cammell Laird shipyards for conversion including a 120ft flying off-deck and accommodation for ten large seaplanes in a hangar below decks.

The *Campania*, commanded by Oliver Schwann, himself a pilot, commenced the working up process of the aircraft carrier, including the launching and recovering of her seaplanes over the side of the ship. A stinging criticism from Admiral Jellicoe in July 1915 regarding the use of aircraft on ships and the fact that not one had ever succeeded in taking off from the *Campania*, caused Oliver Schwann to 'take up the cudgel'. Taking one of the Short 184 seaplanes and placing it on a wheeled trolley, he had the Campania turned into the wind and steaming at 17 knots. Using every inch of the 120ft deck Schwann just managed to get the aircraft airborne. He had proved his point and the *Campania* was returned to Cammell Laird to have the flight deck extended to 200ft.

In March 1916, seaplanes from the seaplane-carriers *Vindex* and *Engadine* made an unsuccessful attack on the Zeppelin sheds at Hoyer in Schleswig, Germany, as the sheds were actually situated nearby at Tondern. A second raid was scheduled for six weeks later and eleven Sopwith Baby fighters, each carrying two bombs, were due to take off from the *Vindex* and the *Engadine*. There were problems from the start – of the eleven that were scheduled for the raid only three managed to get airborne, and of those three only one managed to find the target, and he missed. It was quite obvious that the Sopwith Baby seaplanes were not suitable for such a raid and a complete re-think was required.

It was not until 9 July 1918 that a successful raid was carried out on the Zeppelin sheds. Six Sopwith Camel fighters took off from the flight-deck of HMS *Furious*. This time the Zeppelin sheds were bombed and the Zeppelins L.54 and L.60 completely destroyed.

At last the *Campania* was ready to take an active part in the fleet and she was just in time. She joined the Grand Fleet at Scapa Flow in the Orkney Islands. Assembling the Fleet had been a problem as Zeppelins occasionally carried out reconnaissance flights in the area and any unusual activity would arouse their suspicions. On 30 May 1916 a German coded wireless message was intercepted and partially de-coded at the Admiralty in London. Sufficient information was gleaned from the text to tell the Admiralty that there were large-scale movements of German warships in the North Sea. The Fleet set sail almost immediately,

Short S.41 about to take off in Weymouth harbour.

but the *Campania* never received the order to 'weigh' and was only told after the Fleet had sailed. Going as fast as she could the *Campania* chased after the fleet but was at least four hours behind. Admiral Jellicoe, realising that the aircraft carrier was now a sitting target for any U-boat, ordered her back to Scapa Flow. The crew could only just sit and wait the outcome of what was to be the last epic naval engagement in history.

Although the Battle of Jutland was won by the British Grand Fleet, the British losses were almost double that of the Germans and was only a victory in the sense that the German High Seas Fleet never sailed again. Would the aircraft from the *Campania* have made any difference to the losses suffered by the Grand Fleet? Who knows? What is known is that the low cloud in the area prevented Zeppelins from taking part, and the aircraft from the *Campania* could have flown below the cloud level and sent back the locations of the German ships which might have reduced the casualty list.

The German Imperial Air Service had improved their fighters in the shape of the Fokker Ein-deckers and Tri-deckers, whilst the RNAS still had the lumbering reconnaissance aircraft that were no match for them. What was needed was a sturdy fighter/bomber and a fighter capable of matching the Fokker. Sopwith produced the Sopwith $1\frac{1}{2}$ Strutter fighter/bomber and the Sopwith Pup fighter. The Sopwith $1\frac{1}{2}$ Strutter had a 0.303 Vickers machine gun capable of firing through the propeller, could carry 65lb bombs internally and could be flown either as a single-seater or a two-seater. The two-seater had an observer who was also armed with a 0.303 Lewis machine gun mounted on a rotatable Scarf ring. The aircraft made its appearance in April 1916 with No.5 Wing at Couderque. Within a matter of days they were in action carrying out bombing raids on Zeppelin sheds at Cognelée, Evere and Berchem Ste Agathe.

The Sopwith Pup made its first appearance with the RNAS with No.1 (N) Wing in September 1916, although it had been in service with the RFC for some time. Within a week it had scored its first victory when, just after a German raid when an *Luft-Verkehrs-Gesellschaft* (LVG) had carried out a raid on Dunkirk, a Sopwith Pup flown by Flt Sub-Lt S.J. Goble, took off in pursuit of the bomber and shot it down.

The success of the Sopwith Pup with the RNAS prompted the Admiralty, in response to a desperate request for help from the Army, to form an additional squadron, No.8 (N) Squadron or 'Naval Eight' as it became known. Based at Vert Galand, Naval Eight began operations in October 1916 and was provided with a variety of aircraft to start but within a very short time was equipped entirely with Sopwith Pups. By January 1917 the squadron had accounted for twenty German aircraft and this at a time when German fighters were beginning to dominate the skies over the Somme. It was around this time that the Sopwith Triplane made its appearance. Supplied to only three RNAS squadrons, Nos 1, 8, and 10, the Triplane accounted for over 100 enemy aircraft between April and July 1917. B Flight of No.10 Squadron, led by Flt Sub-Lt Raymond Collishaw, consisted of five Triplanes named *Black Sheep*, *Black Prince*, *Black Roger*, *Black Maria* and *Black Death* and between them they accounted for eighty-seven German aircraft between May and July 1917, Collishaw claiming sixteen of the aircraft within a twenty-seven day period. As the war progressed, Admiral Beatty, who had replaced Admiral Jellicoe in January 1917 as Naval Commander-in-Chief, set up his own Grand Fleet Aeronautical Committee. They immediately formed the opinion that the RNAS was not going to be a supplement to the RFC, but was to be a force within its own right. Three more seaplane carriers were ordered and all were converted steamers. They were the *Pegasus*, *Manxman* and *Nairana*. In addition twenty more Sopwith Pup fighters

Felixstowe F2A. flying boat on its beaching trolley.

were ordered plus twenty two-seater reconnaissance/fighter/bombers. The only problem with these three ships was that all were seaplane carriers and only the *Campania* was built to enable aircraft to take off from its deck. Taking off from the deck of the *Campania* was not a problem, but recovering the aircraft was. It was decided to use a commandeered Italian liner the *Conte Rosso*, which was on the stocks at a British shipyard and turn her into an aircraft carrier with a flush deck. She was renamed HMS *Argus* and launched on 15 August 1916, but not ready for service until June 1917.

Admiral Beatty, although delighted with *Argus*, was not prepared to wait a further year before it could join the Fleet and ordered that the cruiser HMS *Furious* be modified. The forward 18in gun and turret were removed and replaced by a wooden planked flying-off deck angled downwards toward the bows. Beneath the deck was an enclosed hangar capable of taking eight seaplanes. The seaplanes were lifted on to the deck by means of a pair of 40ft derricks mounted either side of a hatch at the aft end of the deck. With the forward gun removed, Beatty decided that if the after turret was removed, the ship would be extremely vulnerable, so it was decided to retain the after turret and its 18in guns.

By June 1917, HMS *Furious* was ready and she was commissioned. Three Short 184 seaplanes with folding wings and five Sopwith Pups that did not have folding wings were placed aboard the ship. It was soon realised that the removal of the Sopwith Pups from the hangar below the deck was going to be a very tricky business as there was virtually no room for error. It was also a manoeuvre that could not safely be carried out in rough weather. Pilots from land bases who flew alongside *Furious*, without exception, made adverse comments on the length of the deck and said that they could see no way of landing on the deck safely. Taking off from the ship was no problem, the *Furious* had a top speed of 31 knots – more than sufficient speed for an aircraft to take off. It was the landings that were the cause for concern. It was decided to carry out a trial landing, after pilots had agreed that if the *Furious* was steaming at 25 knots into a headwind, then it was possible that an aircraft could affect a landing. On 2 August 1917, Sopwith Pup N6452, was made ready with a rope toggle under

A Sopwith Pup being transported on a pontoon out to the seaplane-carrier HMS Furious. It was in this aircraft that Sqn Cdr Dunning lost his life attempting to land on the deck of HMS Furious.

each wing. The pilot, Sqn Cdr Dunning, took off from the ship, circled once and then made his approach to the deck. As he touched down, fellow pilots on the deck grabbed at the toggles and struggled to hold the aircraft down. Dunning switched off the engine and stepped out, the first pilot to land an aircraft on a moving ship. Despite all the accolades, Dunning was not satisfied and decided to make another landing attempt.

The second one took place on 7 August 1917 and again Dunning touched down on the deck, only this time he damaged the elevators on his aircraft in doing so. Climbing out of the Sopwith Pup, he made his way over to another Pup and climbed in, saying he wanted another try. After taking off and circling the ship, he made his approach, only this time he was too high. Dunning waved the deck party to stay clear and opened the throttle to go round again, but the engine stalled and the aircraft fell to the deck, then cartwheeled over the side and into the sea. It is thought that Dunning must have hit his head on the instrument panel and knocked himself unconscious. The floatation bag in the aircraft's tail kept the tail above water, but the remainder of the aircraft was below the surface and Dunning drowned. The result was, that all landings on HMS *Furious* were banned and all subsequent flights resulted in the aircraft either landing ashore or ditching in the water.

A suggestion was put forward to the Admiralty that the aft gun turret be removed and a landing deck installed. The captain of HMS *Furious*, Capt. Wilmot Nicholson, sent the following telegram to the Admiralty:

To Admiralty
Captain of HMS Furious *represents that a flying-on-deck is most undesirable owing to the following reasons:*
(1) Eddy currents aft render landing more dangerous than forward.
(2) Great difficulty and delay in transporting machines from aft forward.
(3) Loss of offensive power owing to after guns having been removed.

A series of five photographs showing the attempted landing and fatal ditching of Sqn Cdr Dunning's aircraft during a failed landing attempt.

> *This question is of vital importance and it is requested that Admiralty officers may be sent up* [to Scapa Flow] *to confer with Captain of HMS* Furious *in order that an immediate decision may be arrived at. There appears to be considerable divergence of opinion on this amongst flying officers.*
> Captain Wilmot Nicholson, R.N.

The Captain's arguments were ignored and the *Furious* was sent to the Newcastle shipyards for the aft gun turret to be removed and an aft flying-on deck to be constructed in its place. Attention then turned to the light cruiser HMS *Yarmouth* which had had a 20ft platform constructed on her forecastle during experiments being carried out on shipborne fighter operations. The first flight was carried out by Lt F.J. Rutland in a Sopwith Camel at the end of June 1917. Then on 21 August 1917, Flt Sub-Lt B.A. Smart made his first take-off in a Sopwith Pup from the deck of HMS *Yarmouth*, and during his test flight encountered the German Zeppelin L.23 and shot it down. Running out of fuel after the encounter, Smart ditched the aircraft in the sea off the Danish coast and was picked up unhurt by the destroyer HMS *Prince*. The Sopwith Pup was abandoned.

Although delighted with the result, the Admiralty realised that there was a problem with launching aircraft from the decks of cruisers and battleships when working with the Fleet – the ship launching the aircraft had to turn into the wind, which sometimes meant that the ship would be pointing in a totally different direction of the rest of the fleet. To attempt to arrest this problem, a 17ft rotatable platform was mounted on top on 'B' turret of HMS *Repulse*, and Sqn Cdr Rutland ran up his engine and flew his Sopwith Pup off the platform with six feet to spare. Another test later proved equally successful, caused the Admiralty to order all light-cruisers and battle-cruisers be fitted with the platform provided they did not interfere with the operation of the guns. Of course the aircraft still had to ditch in the sea beside their ships and be recovered in the normal way.

With the modifications to the flying-off deck of HMS *Furious* almost complete, 284ft long, 'the powers that be' suddenly decided that it might be a shade too short. Experiments were hurriedly carried out using the same techniques used by Eugene Ely when he landed on the USS *Pennsylvania*. After trialling a number of different methods, using a prototype Sopwith Pup, the method accepted was sprung skids, replacing the wheeled undercarriage, with hooks to engage the fore and aft wires running the length of the flight deck. Sopwith Pups destined for shipboard duties were all fitted with the new undercarriage.

The newly modified HMS *Furious* left the shipyards, with Rear Admiral P.F. Phillimore, the Admiral Commanding Aviation, aboard. After taking ten Sopwith Pups and fourteen Sopwith $1\frac{1}{2}$ Strutters on board, HMS *Furious* headed for Scapa Flow to carry out trials on the new flight deck. They were a disaster! Hot funnel gases together with violent eddies and partial vacuums caused tremendous turbulence over the deck, putting even some of the most experienced pilots over the side of the ship – fortunately without serious incident. In the words of Lt W.G. Moore, one of the pilots, 'They just dropped on the deck like shot partridges.'

Further landing trials were abandoned and the pilots reverted back to ditching in the sea. All the time and money spent in modifying HMS *Furious* had been wasted, because she was no better equipped to launch and recover aircraft than those battle-cruisers that had a small platform on top of their gun turrets. Then on 1 April 1918 – April Fool's Day (some say it turned out to be a self-fulfilling prophecy) – control of the Royal Naval Air Service was

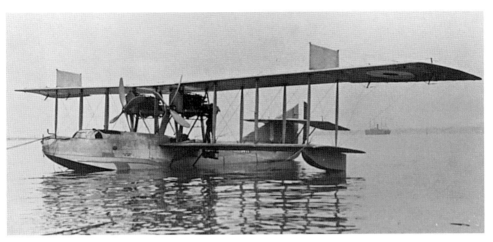

Curtiss H.12 Large American off Killingholme.

Supermarine Seagull N.158 taxiing in Southampton Water.

Curtiss H.12 landing on the River Tay, Dundee, Scotland.

Sopwith 2F1 Camel N.6606 Shall Us *being hoisted aboard the battleship HMS* Renown.

handed over to the newly created independent Air Force. This in fact combined the Royal Flying Corps and Royal Naval Air Service into the Royal Air Force.

The RFC were without doubt the ones who gained in this merger, because the RFC up to this point had mainly relied on the Royal Aircraft Factory for their aircraft development and supply. Now they had a surplus of 2,949 RNAS aircraft, 103 airships, 67,000 officers and men who manned 126 naval air stations, to supplement their badly decimated squadrons at the front. The Navy, when they had purchased aircraft, did so from a variety of manufacturers and had collaborated closely with them. By doing so they were able to spread their requirements across a wide area. In reality, though, there was little change – the uniforms remained the same, the ranks remained the same, the only difference was that the post occupied by the Fifth Sea Lord was abolished and the RNAS came under the control of the newly formed Air Ministry.

On 17 July 1918 'Force A', comprising HMS *Furious* escorted by eight destroyers of the 13th Flotilla and by the 1st Light Cruiser Squadron, left Rosyth to carry out the RAF's first and last shipborne aircraft operation of the war. Seven Sopwith Camels aboard the *Furious* were readied for an attack on the Zeppelin sheds at Tondern, Denmark. The first flight took off, led by Capt. W.D. Jackson, formed up over the fleet, followed moments later by the second flight led by Capt. B.A. Smart. The two flights set a course for Tondern, eighty miles away, when one of the aircraft had engine trouble and had to set down on the water, the pilot was rescued by a British destroyer. The remaining six aircraft continued, then as they approached Sylt, the two flights split so as to make individual attacks form different directions on the Zeppelin sheds. Just north of Tondern the giant sheds suddenly sprang into view and the attack began. Despite withering rifle and machine gun fire, the first flight bombed one of the sheds setting it on fire and destroying two Zeppelins, L.54 and L.60 inside. The second flight bombed and completely destroyed the second shed. Two of the Sopwith Pups ran out of petrol and had to carry out emergency landings in Denmark, another made a navigational error and had to land at Ringkobing, just twenty miles east of the Fleet. Lt W.A. Yeulett went missing and was presumed to have crashed into the sea and was lost, whilst Capts. Smart and Dickson ditched alongside the Fleet and were picked up. The mission was a success despite losing one pilot and all but one of the aircraft.

Three weeks later, during an experiment where a Sopwith Camel was on a lighter being towed behind a destroyer, a Zeppelin appeared in the distance. The pilot of the Camel, Lt S.D. Culley, signalled the destroyer to increase speed and then took off the lighter in pursuit of the Zeppelin. Climbing to 19,000ft Culley made his attack and shot down Zeppelin.

At the end of September the converted ex-Italian liner *Conte Rosso*, having been subjected to further modifications after the disastrous experiments aboard HMS *Furious*, joined the Fleet as HMS *Argus*. She now had a 576ft long flush deck from the bows to the stern, she was the first true aircraft carrier. The ship was controlled from a small charthouse which was raised hydraulically above the flight deck when required for navigation purposes and lowered when the carrier was launching and recovering her aircraft.

The first launch and recovery of an aircraft from the deck of HMS *Argus* was carried out by Cdr Richard Bell Davis in October 1918, when he flew his Sopwith 1½ Strutter off the deck and carried out a landing using the longitudinal wires to stop his aircraft. Sopwith T1 Cuckoos were placed aboard the *Argus* making her operational, but the following month came Armistice and peace. The Naval air arm had without question played a major part in the war and left an indelible mark on the future of naval aviation.

A rare air-to-air shot of a Short 320 on patrol in the North Sea.

RNAS Aircraft of the First World War

Avro 504

Beardmore W.B.IV
Blackburn Blackbird
Blackburn Kangaroo
Bristol Scout
Bristol T.B.8

D.H.2
D.H.4

Fairey Campania
Fairey Hamble Baby
Fairey IIIC
Felixstowe F.2A

Grain Kitten

Handley Page 0/100
Handley Page 0/400

Mann Egerton H.1

Pemberton–Billing P.B.25
Port Victoria P.V.7
Port Victoria P.V.9

S.E.5a
Short 184
Short 320
Short 827
Short 830
Short Bomber
Short M.2
Short S.26
Short S.28
Short S.38
Short Tandem Twin 8
Sopwith 1½ Strutter
Sopwith Admiralty Type 807
Sopwith Bat Boat
Sopwith Camel
Sopwith Pup
Sopwith Tabloid
Sopwith Triplane

Vickers F.B.5. Gunbus

Wright Converted Seaplane

Sopwith 2F1 Camel aboard the cruiser HMS Calliope.

Curtiss H.4 flying boat 'Small America' at RNAS Killingholme.

Short Admiralty Type 827 No.3326 having just landed in the sea off Calshot.

Bristol Scout C of A Flight No.3 Wing RNAS at Thasos, Greece, preparing to take-off.

Flt Sub-Lt Le Mesurier seen here in an early Blériot of the RNAS.

This photograph is said to show Flt Cdr B.D. Kilner in his Sopwith Pup taking off from HMS Vindex in pursuit of a Zeppelin. He was never seen again.

Officers of No.1 Wing RNAS (Nos 2(N) & 3(N) Squadrons). Top, from left: Bette, Alexander, Nelson, Richardson, White, Wambolt, Beamish, Hosketh, Powell, Pierce, Wg-Off Berry, and Wg-Off England. Middle, from left: Wyatt, Mack, Smilie, MacNab, Mulock, Wg Cdr Chambers, Sqn Cdr Evill, Greenwood, Edwards, Furhiss, and Traynor. Front, from left: Gow, Chase, Travers, Holder, Tapscott, and Griffen.

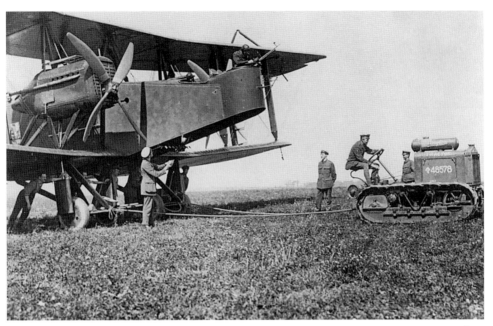

Handley Page 0/400 night bomber being towed into position for take off by a RNAS tractor and ground crew.

Flt Cdr Babbington and Flt Lt Sippe being decorated with the Legion of Honour and the Cross of the Order by General Thévenet, the Governor of the fortress of Belfont, for their part in the raid on the Zeppelin sheds at Friedrichshafen.

The window of the London store of Robinson & Cleaver, suppliers of uniforms to the RNAS and RFC.

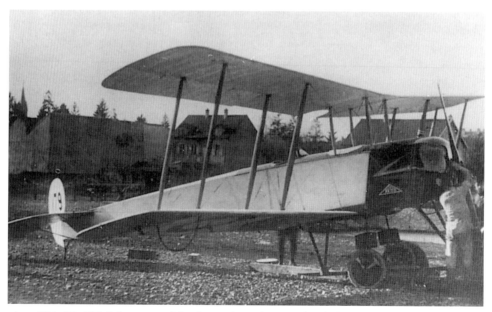

Avro 504, No.179, being prepared for the attack on the Zeppelin sheds at Friedrichshafen. This aircraft broke a tail skid on take-off and took no part in the raid.

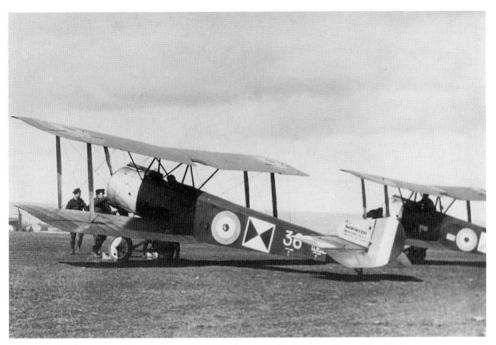

Sopwith 1½ Strutter on No.3 Wing RNAS at Luxeuil des Baines, France, in 1917.

SS.ZB leaving to go on patrol.

North Sea airship about to leave on patrol.

SS.Z airship on patrol in the English Channel.

Coastal Class airship escorting a convoy of merchant ships.

Convoy of merchant ships entering the English Channel under the watchful eye of an RNAS airship.

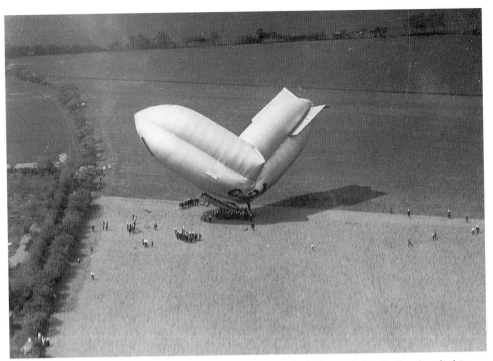

The RNAS airship C.21 comes to grief after hitting the roof of a hut as it lifted off and gashed its gas envelope, 1 June 1918.

SS.Z airship down amongst the trees at Johnstown Castle, Co. Wexford.

4
United States Naval and Marine Corps Air Services

When the United States entered the war in 1917, the principle role of the Navy was that of guardian of the seas, but a new branch was growing from within its various branches – aviation. Interest in aviation had started as far back as the American Civil War, when both the Union and Confederacy successfully launched observation balloons from surface vessels. In 1898, the then Assistant Secretary of the Navy, Theodore Roosevelt, tried to get support for Samuel P. Langley's unsuccessful 'Aerodrome' flying machine, but to the military hierarchy it remained merely a secondary interest. Even with the support of Admiral George Dewey, the acclaimed hero of the Battle of Manilla Bay, who decided to carry out experiments on using the aeroplane as an observation platform, the interest still waned very quickly. But there was still within the navy a dedicated group of officers who saw a future in aviation.

As part of Fleet manoeuvres in January 1913, an aviation camp was set up on Fisherman's Point, Guantanamo Bay, Cuba. The aircraft flew scouting missions and carried out spotting sorties for mines and submerged submarines. So successful were they that a great deal of general interest was generated in this new addition to the Navy's operational capabilities, but a major influential interest was still missing. But the die-hards in the Navy persisted and in January 1914, Naval Air Station Pensacola, Florida, was set up, even though naval aviation was still being regarded by many to be just a passing phase. It soon became obvious that the training of the air and ground crews at Pensacola had no sense of discipline or purpose behind it and that the air crews consisted mainly of graduates from Annapolis. The curriculum at the time covered only the technical side of aviation, and for some unknown reason, omitted fundamental navigation and seamanship.

But in April 1914, the rumblings of a revolution in Mexico, precipitated by the arrest of three American sailors at Tampico, reared its head again – only this time it was the US Navy who were involved. The first message that mobilised the Naval Aviation section into action was sent to Pensacola on Sunday 19 April 1914. It was sent to Capt. William Sims whilst he was having lunch aboard the Aeronautical Training Ship, the cruiser USS *Birmingham*, with the captain of the ship Lt Cdr Henry 'Rum' Mustin. The message read:

DIRECT COMMANDING OFFICER AERONAUTIC STATION REPORT YOU FOR SERVICE ONE AEROPLANE SECTION CONSISTING TWO FLYING BOATS OR HYDROAEROPLANES ONE SPARE BOAT OR PONTOON TWO SPARE MOTORS TWO HANGARS TENTAGE FOR PERSONAL AND OTHER NECESSARY SPARES AND OUTFITS. LIEUTENANT TOWERS IN CHARGE WITH LIEUTENANT SMITH AND ENSIGN CHEVALIER AND TEN MECHANICIENS.

Lt Cdr Mustin went on deck to inspect the facilities required for such a mission. The USS *Birmingham* had been in the public's eye on 14 November 1910, when Eugene Ely had flown a Curtiss pusher from her deck, only this time aircraft were going to have to fly from her deck under battle conditions. If successful, it would be a great boost for naval aviation, if not it could spell the death knell. After his initial inspection, Mustin realised that the ship had no facilities for hoisting the aircraft in or out of the water. Lowering booms were quickly installed on the mainmast to serve as derricks.

The situation in Mexico suddenly reached its climax, when a message was received in Washington that a German merchant ship was to dock on 21 April at Veracruz, with a cargo of weapons and ammunition for Gen. Victoria Huerta's troops.

The USS *Birmingham*, with an aviation detachment aboard consisting of three pilots, three aircraft and twelve enlisted men, all under the command of Lt John H. Towers, was immediately dispatched to join the Atlantic Fleet forces operating off the coast of Tampico. Meanwhile, the USS *Mississippi*, under the command of Rear Admiral Frank Jack Fletcher, with a second aviation detachment aboard, was dispatched to assist in the military operations at Veracruz. On 21 April 1914, the Fleet landing force lost nineteen men to snipers from the revolutionary army, when they attempted to seize Veracruz.

The city was a contrast of extremes. The pastel-painted buildings with their green and pink balconies set against a background of deep azure blue skies, presented a beautiful sight. But the reality was that the vast majority of the city had no sanitation, disease was rampant and

Eugene Ely's Curtiss Pusher being serviced aboard the light cruiser USS Birmingham *in the Norfolk Navy Yard.*

the whole area reeked repulsively of rotting refuse and human waste. This cesspit of a city was what the US Navy and Marines were about to try and take.

The USS *Mississippi*, launched its first observation flight, an AB-3 flying boat flown by Lt (junior grade - jg) P.N.L. Bellinger ★, over the harbour of Veracruz to search for mines. Two days later a second flight was made to photograph the harbour, again by Bellinger but this time accompanied by an observer, Ensign W.D. LaMont.

On 2 May 1914, the USS *Mississippi* launched a third flight, this time in a Curtiss C-3 (AH-3) floatplane, to search for enemy troops reported near Tejar. After flying for over fifty minutes they returned to the ship having seen nothing but American Army troops – they had, however, recorded the first American aerial mission under military conflict conditions. Four days later, 6 May 1914, Bellinger, with Lt (jg) Saufley as observer ★★, flew a reconnaissance flight over enemy positions near Veracruz. Their aircraft was hit by rifle fire from the 'invisible' enemy – the first marks of combat on a US Naval aircraft.

Over the next few days, the two men carried out several more observation flights over the town, more as a show of strength than a serious threat, but fortunately without further incident. The flights were merely token gestures in support of the 'bluejackets' who were already in the town mopping up what was left of the resistance.

An aviation camp was set up on the beach and the work of scouting the area continued. After flying a number of missions during the next month with no results, the number of flights were reduced to one a day. The crews of the aircraft were looking for ghosts and they knew it. The Navy felt that it was a waste of time and effort to continue, but were told that they would have to stay until the Army was able to get some of their Air Service aircraft there. No.1 Aero Squadron had been dispatched to aid the navy, but by the time they reached Fort Crocket, near Galveston, Texas, the incident in Mexico was virtually over and the squadron, together with its uncrated aircraft, returned to San Diego.

This in reality made a nonsense of the attempt to provide air support for ground troops, and highlighted the lack of commitment at the time by the American government to the future of air power. Subsequently, however, it did spur the manufacturers of aircraft (only twelve manufacturers were deemed to be capable of producing what could loosely be called military aircraft) to look into the problem seriously. Four hundred aircraft were produced during 1916, and not one could be considered to be a pure military aircraft.

Endnotes

★ Bellinger later commanded one of the four NC aircraft, the NC-1, in the US Navy's successful attempt to fly the Atlantic, although only one, the NC-4, was to complete the trip. Bellinger became an Admiral in the Second World War.

★★ Lt (jg) Saufley was to lose his life in an AH-9, on 9 June 1916, when his aircraft crashed into the sea off Santa Rosa Island, Pensacola. It happened during an endurance flight after the aircraft had been in the air for 8 hours and 51 minutes. The cause is not known, but was possibly engine failure.

Left and below:
Eugene Ely making the first landing aboard a ship. Seen here about to touch down on the deck of the cruiser USS Pennsylvania *in a Curtiss biplane.*

5
United States Navy and Marine Corps Prepare for War

On the declaration of war against Germany, US naval aviation strength stood at thirty-eight officers and 163 enlisted men, all with aviation experience of one kind and another. They had fifty-four aircraft (some were shared with the Marine Corps) – all of them training types, one free balloon, one kite balloon, one very suspect dirigible and one air station. The Navy had started training pilots and crews some six years earlier, but it had fallen off over the last year, mainly because of the number of accidents they had had. This was not the fault of the instructors or students in the main, but of the aircraft themselves. It has to be remembered that the aircraft industry in America, like its counterparts in Europe, was still at the fledgling stage of its development and some of their aircraft left a lot to be desired. The main source of aircraft came from abroad, mainly Britain and France.

Over $3 million had been set aside for the US Navy's Naval Flying Corps, as it was known in the Naval Appropriation Act of 29 August 1916; unfortunately, for one reason or another, none of the funding appeared to find its way into the Navy's coffers. Although the Naval Flying Corps had not yet been officially established, an aviation desk had been set up in the Office of the Chief of Naval Operations and a Lt Jack Towers was recalled from attaché duty in London to take control of it. Because of his rank, Towers soon found himself in difficulty when dealing with the bureaucracy that surrounded him. A promotion to Lieutenant Commander did nothing to ease the situation, and it was realised that if the 'desk' was to survive, then a more senior officer would be required. In May 1917, Capt. Noble E. 'Bull' Irwin was appointed to the post and, although he was not an aviator, he saw that there was a real future in naval aviation and gave Towers his full support. Suitable sites for air bases had been selected along the East Coast, but all were still in the planning stages. Late in 1916 the first of the Curtiss N-9s had been delivered to the Navy and experiments were started with shipboard catapults aboard the USS *North Carolina*, the USS *Huntingdon* and the USS *Seattle*.

In Britain, France, Germany, Italy and the Austro-Hungarian Empire, naval aviation was being actively encouraged, leaving the United States woefully behind. But interest was growing, and a number of wealthy young men at the various universities in America decided to buy their own aircraft and hire instructors to teach them. F. Trubee Davison of Yale University formed the First Yale Unit, which was later incorporated into the Aerial Coastal Patrol Unit No.1. This unit was the brainchild of Rear Admiral Robert E. Peary and Henry Woodhouse, both ardent believers in naval aviation, who raised money from individual contributions to form the National Coastal Patrol Commission. This encouraged Curtiss and other enterprising manufacturers to set up flying training schools, not only for pilots, but for mechanics and engineers to keep the aircraft flying.

Although Davison had a number of students at Yale ready to learn to fly, he still had the problem of finding enough aircraft and instructors to meet their needs. Just outside New York on Long Island, a Philadelphia merchant by the name of Rodman Wanamaker operated a flying school at Port Washington. After long consultations with him, Davison managed to persuade him to let them use one Curtiss Flying Boat and an instructor named David McCulloch. McCulloch was later to gain fame as the co-pilot of the NC-3 flying boat on the US Navy's successful attempt to become the first to fly the Atlantic Ocean – only one of the four NC aircraft, the NC-4. The summer of 1917 saw the first twelve members of the First Yale Unit at Locust Valley clambering all over their Curtiss flying boat – maintaining it, cleaning it and learning to fly. By the end of the summer four of the students had flown solo and the remaining eight were ready to do so. Toward the end of the year the students were invited to take part, as members of the Aerial Coastal Patrol, in manoeuvres off Sandy Hook with battleships, destroyers and coastal boats. The military and civilian observers were so impressed with the standard of flying by the Yale faculty during the highly successful manoeuvres that they gave them two more seaplanes and additional funding.

In March 1917 the whole unit was transferred to West Palm Beach, Florida, to take advantage of the weather and to finalise the remaining of their flying training. All members of the First Yale Unit were enrolled into the US Navy and a naval lieutenant placed in command. One month later the unit returned to Long Island and began the business of flight training in readiness for war.

Ironically, Trubee Davison never qualified as a pilot – he was injured when his aircraft crashed on his final examination flight. In 1966, on the fiftieth anniversary of the Naval Air Reserve, Trubee Davison was awarded his wings as an Honorary Aviator, a fitting tribute to a man who was a tremendous influence on the birth of US naval aviation.

On 7 April 1917, the President directed that control of the US Coast Guard be transferred from the Treasury department to the US Navy. Later the same month was the formation of the Marine Aeronautic Company, Advance Base Force, at the Marine barracks in the Philadelphia Navy Yard, under the command of Capt. A.A. Cunningham. The company was made up from the Marine Aviation Section at Pensacola and from the Marine Corps Reserve Flying Corps, and had a complement of thirty-four officers and 330 enlisted men.

The US Marine Corps had not been idle, and aviation essentially started for them on 22 May 1912, when the first Marine aviator, 1st Lt A.A. Cunningham reported for his initial

NAS Pensacola with three Curtiss H-12 flying boats on the slipway.

A Curtiss H-16 flying boat entering the water for the first United States Navy flight from Ireland.

flight training at Annapolis, Maryland. After receiving his ground instruction, Cunningham was posted to the Burgess Co. and Curtiss Aircraft Factory at Marblehead, Massachusetts, for flight training itself. On 1 August 1912, after two hours of training he flew solo, even though he had only witnessed two landings prior to his own. Cunningham became Marine Aviator No.1 and designated Naval Aviator No.5. Two more Marines followed that year, Lt Bernard L. Smith and 2nd Lt William M. McLivain. But it wasn't until June 1915 that the next marine, 1st Lt Francis T. Evans, reported for training, followed on 31 March 1916 by 1st Lt Roy Geiger. These five marine aviators were to form the nucleus of USMC Aviation.

Both Smith and Cunningham contributed enormously to the experimental and development phases of Marine Corps aviation, although they had different concepts on how the aviation side should be used. Cunningham favoured total support of the Marine Corps, whereas Smith saw Marine Corps aviation supporting both the Navy and the Corps. During January and February 1914, Smith, and 2nd Lt McLivain, who the following year became Marine Aviator No.3, together with ten enlisted mechanics, one flying boat and one amphibian, were involved in a combined fleet and landing force exercise at Culebra, Puerto Rico. The two pilots flew daily missions over the island, carrying brigade officers to show them the ease, speed and field of vision that aerial reconnaissance offered. The aviation contribution to the exercise was a complete success. So much so, that Lt Smith's recommendation that an advanced base consisting of five aviators and twenty enlisted ground crewmen be set up, was taken up by the Marine Corps.

As the year progressed the Marine Aeronautic Company, as it was collectively known, was divided into two units. They were the 1st Marine Aeronautic Company, consisting of ten officers and ninety-three men, and would prepare for seaplane missions, whilst the other, the 1st Aviation Squadron, consisting of twenty-four officers and 237 men, would support the Marine brigade in France. On 14 October 1917 the 1st Marine Aeronautic Company, under the command of Capt. Francis T. Evans, USMC, was posted to Navy Coastal Air Station Cape May, New Jersey, for extensive seaplane training and, ultimately, coastal patrol. By the end of the year the squadron was ready to embark aboard the USS *Hancock* for Ponta Delgada in the Azores. With them they took ten Curtiss R-6 seaplanes, two N-9 seaplanes and six Curtiss HS-2-1 flying boats. They were the first fully trained and equipped flying unit to be stationed overseas.

The cruiser USS Huntington *with its kite balloon aloft and a Curtiss N-9H aboard.*

The squadron carried out patrols around the waters that surrounded the islands from dawn to dusk and the only sighting they had of the enemy was on 11 September 1918. A Curtiss R-6 was on patrol with pilot Lt Walter Poague and Gy Sgt Zeigler, when they sighted a German U-boat on the surface. They circled, then came in to attack and dropped their one and only bomb. Unfortunately not only did the bomb miss, but it also failed to explode and the two flyers could only watch as the submarine's crew leisurely battened down the hatches and then submerged out of sight.

But the squadron maintained constant patrols from Ponta Delgada throughout the war, their very presence caused the enemy to become very careful and the squadron served with great distinction.

The second unit from within the 1st Aviation Force, the 1st Aviation Squadron under the command of Capt. McIlvain, was sent from Philadelphia to the Army Aviation School at Hazelhurst Field, Mineola, Long Island, New York, for basic training. Because of the increasing inclement weather, the whole squadron was moved to the Army's Gerstner Field at Lake Charles, Louisiana.

A detachment from within the 1st Aviation Force was formed under the command of Capt. Roy Geiger, USMC. This unit, consisting of four officers and thirty-six enlisted men, was ordered to Miami, Florida, where they took over a small airfield owned by the Curtiss Flying School. After extensive training and the influx of a number of fully trained pilots from the US Navy, the First Marine Aviation Force was mobilised for France and its first taste of war. On 1 April 1918 Capt. McIlvain's squadron arrived in Florida to join up with Capt. Geiger's squadron. The nucleus of the 1st Aviation Force was all together for the first time in one location. The force was then shaped into four squadrons, designated A, B, C and D.

6
United States Navy and Marine Corps in the First World War

The US Marines entered the war under the direction of Maj.-Gen. Commandant George Barnett. Initially the Marines were to send a brigade to fight alongside the Army, but with the advent of Marine Aviation, another string to the Marines' bow was created. The 1st Marine Aeronautic Company was already in action in the Azores, when the First Marine Aviation Force sailed for France on 18 July 1918 aboard the USS *De Kalb*. Upon landing in France on 30 July, the force disembarked at Brest and travelled the 400 miles to their base at Calais by a requisitioned train. After a long delay, when it was discovered that there were no aircraft available for the Marines, they were assigned to fly with British crews whilst arrangements were made for the supply of aircraft. On 12 October the force joined the Day Wing of the Northern Bombing Group with their own aircraft and although their time was limited before the Armistice was signed, they carried out a number of important bombing raids. One raid in particular, on 14 October 1918, concerned eight DH-4s on a bombing mission to carry out a raid on the German-held railway yards at Thielt, Belgium. On the way back from the raid, which was not very successful, the formation was jumped by twelve German fighters. One of the bombers was separated from the others and singled out for attack. The gunner, Gy Sgt Robert G. Robinson managed to shoot down one of the attackers before he himself was hit. Despite his wounds Robinson continued to fight whilst

The United States Naval Air Station at Killingholme being officially handed over to the US Navy.

Assembling a Curtiss H-16 flying boat at United States Naval Air Station, Brest, on 2 November 1918.

his pilot, 2nd Lt Ralph Talbot, weaved all over the sky. Robinson was hit twice more and was rendered unconscious. Talbot shot down another of the fighters with his fixed guns and then decided that discretion was the better part of valour and put his aircraft into a steep dive. Levelling off at an altitude of 50ft, Talbot roared over the German lines and landed safely at a Belgian airfield, where his gunner was taken to hospital for treatment. Robinson recovered and together with Talbot, was awarded America's highest accolade – the Medal of Honour. Talbot was killed on 26 October 1918, carrying out an engine test on an old worn-out DH.4. The engine failed on take-off with the result that the aircraft plunged into the ground and exploded into flames on contact.

During the relatively short period of time that US Marine Aviation was involved in the war, they carried out fifty-seven missions, dropped a total of 33,932lb of bombs, at a cost of four pilots killed, one pilot and two gunners wounded. They accounted for four German fighters and claimed eight more possibles.

Whilst the Marine Corps were getting to grips with their new squadrons, the Navy was showing increasing interest in the use of airships for coastal patrol duties. On 30 May 1917 the first flight of the Navy's first airship, a B-Class model, was successful after making the trip from Chicago, where it was made, to Akron, Ohio. It was flown by a Goodyear pilot by the name of R.H. Upson. A second flight in the airship, designated DN-1 by the Navy and flown by LCDR Frank R. McCrary, USN, was made from Pensacola, but was a dismal failure. Even after extensive alterations and testing, the results were the same and only two more flights followed before the airship was finally grounded for the last time. But the lighter-than-air programme supported by the Goodyear Tire & Rubber Co. was slowly gaining momentum. Goodyear had agreed with the Navy that they would provide the facilities and the equipment and all the Navy had to do was to provide the trainees. The school opened on a field located at Fritsche's Lake (later called Wingfoot), three miles from the town of Akron. It consisted of a hangar, 400ft x 100ft x 100ft, tool and equipment shops, classrooms, barracks for the students and quarters for the officers. Within six months the first eight men had qualified and were designated Naval Aviators (Dirigibles), but it was to be a further two months before they were assigned to their units. Another training base was set up later at Pensacola, Florida. Contracts to five different companies had been awarded for sixteen new B-Class airships, all based on a similar design and to the specifications laid down by the Navy. As crews became more competent, coastal patrols from naval air stations were commenced. The airships operated from Naval Air Stations at Chatham, Massachusetts; Cape May, New Jersey; Rockaway Beach and Montauk Point, New York; and Key West, Florida. Although the airships that carried out these coastal patrols proved to be an extremely useful weapon, it was not one ever used in Europe. Trained LTA (Lighter Than Air) pilots were sent to NAS Paimbœuf in France, where they carried out familiarisation training in French airships before going on active service patrols.

The use of manned kite balloons on battleships and destroyers for observation purposes, was a direct spin-off from the airships. These balloons, unlike the airships, were tethered to the ships and had no directional movement, other than up and down, save that of the ships own movement. Their purpose was to spot enemy warships or submarines, but they were controlled by the weather. If the seas were relatively calm, then the observation kite balloon was launched, but if there were high seas running or it was foggy then it was impracticable.

Experiments were also started with a guided-missile programme after funding of $50,000 had been allocated by the Secretary of the Navy. The work centred around the use of aerial torpedoes in the form of automatic gyroscopically-controlled aircraft. The results were at first encouraging, but the longer they went on the more expensive they got, and the project was shelved. It was resurrected during the Second World War but then only used on a couple of occasions.

The first national insignia designed for United States aircraft was ordered to be placed on all Naval aircraft. It was a red disc within a white star on a blue circular field on the wings,

United States Naval Air Station, Queenstown, southern Ireland.

and red, white and blue vertical stripes with blue forward on the rudder. One of the main reasons for the insignia was the increasing number of incidents where US aircraft were fired upon by their own troops and it was deemed to be necessary to educate the ground troops in the, then, simplest way.

At the end of May 1917 a second Yale unit was formed under the leadership of Ganson Goodyear Depew of Buffalo, New York. He presented the idea of the new unit to Admiral W.S. Benson who was CNO (Chief of Naval Operations) at the time. The twelve members of the unit were enlisted into the USNRF (United States Naval Reserve Force) and ordered to report to Lt Wadleigh Capehart at Buffalo, New York. As was seemed to be the practice at the time, most of the funding came from private sources, and equipment, together with a second-hand Curtiss F boat, was purchased. The existence of the Second Yale Unit, or Aerial Coastal Patrol Unit No.2 as it became known, was very nearly cut short when, on one of the first excursions of the one and only, newly-acquired Curtiss flying boat, it crashed, killing the instructor, Fred Zimmer. The crash also injured the passenger, Seymour Knox, so badly that he was invalided out of the war. Ganson Depew acquired another aircraft and flying instructor at his own expense and persuaded the Naval authorities to give them another chance, which fortunately they did.

The trust that the Naval Board had bestowed upon them bore fruit when in the November, all twelve passed the stringent tests required to gain their 'Wings of Gold'. The final flying test was to take the Curtiss F flying boat up to 6,000ft, cut the engine and glide down in a spiral, then land on the water and taxi to a point not less than 20ft from a marker buoy. Three students actually stopped with their aircraft's nose nestling against the buoy. The twelve were granted commissions as Ensigns and five were posted overseas to Europe, six to NAS Pensacola and one to Washington DC After arriving in Europe the five new Ensigns were posted to Moutchic, France, for bombing instruction in French FBA flying boats. Later the same month three of them were posted to RNAS Felixstowe, where they were introduced to the delights of the twin-engined F2A flying boat.

It was at Felixstowe in November 1917 that they took part in 'lighter stunt' experiments with the F2A flying boat. This was developed from the need to carry out long-range reconnaissance flights over the North Sea. The distance from Felixstowe to the Danish coastline of Heligoland was 340 miles, and because the aircraft did not have this kind of range, the aircraft could not spot German shipping making journeys northwards up the coast of Denmark.

Wg Capt. C.R. Sansom, RN, and Wg Cdr Porte, RFC, developed a 'lighter' that could carry an F2A flying boat and be towed behind a destroyer at high speed. The 'lighter' was in fact a barge that settled quite low in the water and was a derivative of the Thames lighter barges that were used to carry materials up and down the Thames.

Three destroyers towing three lighters with F2As aboard left Felixstowe and proceeded across the North Sea to a point near the Dutch coast. The aircraft were off-loaded from the lighters and then took off on patrol. The three aircraft flew along the coast to the Bight of Heligoland, then back across the North Sea to Felixstowe and returned safely. A number of flights were made using this system and all were very successful. The other two Ensigns who were still in France, were assigned to the NBG (Northern Bombing Group) and carried out ferry flights of Caproni bombers from Italy over the Alps to northern France. These were hair-raising flights as the reliability of these aircraft was always being brought into question.

Among the three Ensigns that went to Felixstowe was Ensign Stephen Potter, who became second pilot to an experienced Canadian pilot by the name of Flt Lt Norman Magor. Potter had specialised in gunnery, using all his spare time on the gunnery range practising a variety of techniques, including the practice of 'leading the target'. In March 1918, while on patrol off the coast of Holland in an F2A, the two aviators were attacked by a German Friedrichshafen FF.29 – Potter's hours of gunnery practice were rewarded when the German aircraft, which flew alongside them trading shots, was shot down. Two weeks later the intrepid two were attacked by seven Brandenburg monoplane seaplanes and, though defending themselves well, they were hopelessly outnumbered and were shot down into the sea. The deaths of Flt Lt Magor and Ensign Potter came as a real blow to the unit, bringing the brutal reality of war home to them all.

The first naval medal of the war for bravery concerned with aviation, albeit indirectly, was awarded to Ship Fitter First Class Patrick McGunigal, USN, for an heroic rescue on 17 September 1917. The incident happened whilst the armoured cruiser USS *Huntington* was escorting an Atlantic convoy to Britain. The cruiser had been fitted with a kite observation balloon and as the convoy and cruiser entered what was deemed to be the war zone, the kite balloon was launched, with its observer Lt (jg) H.W. Hoyt, USN, aboard. The temperature suddenly dropped and the balloon rapidly lost height just as a squall hit. The balloon was rapidly pulled in, but Hoyt and the basket were dragged beneath the waves. Patrick McGunigal immediately dived over the side of the ship and scrambled down the ropes to the basket. After managing to extricate Hoyt from a tangled mass of ropes, he brought him to the surface, tied a bowline around him and watched as he was hauled aboard the cruiser. Then McGunigal allowed himself to be hauled aboard. For this rescue he was awarded the Medal of Honor.

Meanwhile in the United Kingdom on 3 July 1918, the United States Navy raised the American flag over the RAF base at Killingholme, Lincolnshire, making NAS Killingholme the largest US naval air station in Europe. Just prior to taking over the station, a Zeppelin was reported heading for the area and two of the American pilots, Ensign Ashton 'Tex'

United States Naval Air Station, Île Tudy, France.

United States Naval Air Station l'Aber Vrach, France, with all its aircraft ready for launching.

W. Hawkins and Lt (jg) G. Francklyn Lawrence, took off in their H.16 flying boat to intercept. After flying through heavy rain and strong winds, Tex Hawkins took the aircraft through the clouds to 10,000ft. There was no moon that night and the two Americans scoured the star filled skies for a sign of the Zeppelin, but to no avail. After several hours of chasing shadows, they descended through the heavy overcast and into heavy fog. Hopelessly lost, they cruised at wave top height until they spotted a line of trawlers heading out to sea. Assuming that the trawlers were going out to sea, they reversed the course the trawlers were taking and headed toward the coast. When a rock breakwater loomed in front of them, they hopped over and landed in a harbour. As they taxied toward the shore line, a seaplane ramp loomed up in front of them, with a black cavernous hangar situated at the end of it. An amazed RNAS ground crew hauled the H.16 up the ramp, whereupon a Royal Navy officer asked how the devil they had managed to find the base in such filthy weather. Tex Hawkins glanced at his co-pilot and with a wink replied, 'The one thing they taught us to do in flight training, Sir, was to navigate', and grinned with obvious relief.

The first contingent of United States Naval Aviators had arrived at Pauillac, France, on 5 June 1917, aboard the converted collier USS *Jupiter* (AC-3). Three days later a second contingent aboard a converted collier, USS *Neptune* (AC-8), landed at St Nazaire, France. The two groups were under the command of a junior officer by the name of Lt Kenneth Whiting, and consisted of seven officers and 122 enlisted men, none of whom had aviation training or experience. Whiting immediately negotiated with the French for accommodation and training, as it was his intention to get his aviators into the fray as quickly as possible. With agreements reached he headed for London and a meeting with Admiral William S. Sims, Commander US Naval Forces Europe, to tell him what he had done. Sims immediately took to the lieutenant's eagerness and sent him back to the United States with a request that Washington establish a training station at Mount Lacanau, near Bordeaux. This was granted and the training establishment was set up, together with operational stations at St Trojan, Dunkirk and Le Croisic. Promoted to Lieutenant Commander, Whiting was replaced by a more senior officer, Capt. Hutchinson Cone, USN, and returned to the United States in January 1918, after having organised the setting up of US Naval Air Stations throughout Europe in conjunction with the Royal Air Force. Through Whiting, the US Navy now had in place the makings of a very respectable force.

One American sailor who remembered his first introduction to flying in the Navy, was Ensign Joe C. Cline. He had enlisted in the United States Navy on 3 April 1917 as a Landsman for Quartermaster (Aviation). He was sent to NAS Pensacola with a number of other eager student aviators for flight training, unfortunately there was no provision for such a large contingent of students at ground school or otherwise. For three weeks the group was drilled and indoctrinated into the naval way of life. This in itself was no hardship for Joe Cline, as he had spent four years in the Illinois Naval Militia prior to joining the Navy. Then, quite suddenly, the group were posted overseas to France. They boarded the USS *Neptune* at Baltimore and with the destroyers USS *Perkins* and USS *Jarvis* as escorts, headed across the Atlantic toward France.

Two days later the group headed for the then small fishing village of Brest and took over what were once the barracks of Napoleon's soldiers. In the meantime Lt Whiting had returned from Paris with an agreement that the French would train them as pilots, supply them with aircraft, engines, fuel, armament and bombs. The group was loaded into trucks and driven to Tours, the home of Ecole d'Aviation Militaire de Tours. They were arranged into groups of eight and each group was assigned to one instructor. One leather flying coat, one pair of goggles and one crash helmet was given to each group, and these were passed from one student to another as and when he came to fly in the school's Caudron G.3.

There was one minor problem, however – the French instructors spoke no English and the American students spoke no French. It was resolved by having paste cards with a line

Aerial view of Brest, France. The United States Naval Air Station can be seen at the bottom centre.

drawn down the middle, with English one side and French the other. After each flight the instructor would point out the mistakes on the paste cards, whilst giving the student a verbal scolding in French. Two thirds of the group managed to solo in after only five hours of instruction, so it said something for the ability of the French instructors and the ingenuity of the American students. On completion of the course, the students were sent to Ecole d'Aviation Maritime de Hourtin based on a small lake outside Bordeaux. It was here that the Americans received their preliminary seaplane training in Franco-British Aviation (FBA). After a month the students were sent to Ecole d'Aviation de St Raphael in the south of France. Here the students were taught to fly a variety of seaplanes, carry out bombing, gunnery courses and to carry out a number of water landings on the sea. Just four months after arriving in France, and with 31 hours and 52 minutes of flying time behind him, Joe Cline received his French brevet. He was later posted to Le Croisic to join pilots of the First Aeronautic Detachment.

At the small villages of Le Croisic by the Loire River, the small US naval air station based there had been operational since October 1917. The building of the station had commenced back on 26 July 1917 and had been built using nineteen German prisoners-of-war. But it wasn't until 29 October before the base was activated, with the arrival from the United States, of three Ensigns (two of whom were pilots), thirteen enlisted men and eleven observers. The first flight from the base was made on 18 November and the US Navy had their first taste of action. They were called to investigate the sighting of a German submarine off the coast and Ensign Kenneth Smith, the pilot, Ensign Frank Brady, observer, and Machinist W.M. Wilkinson clambered aboard their newly-arrived Tellier flying boat and took off with a bomb under each wing. Dawn had only just broken, but by the end of the day they still had not returned. The following day, as soon as it was light, the other flight crews were scrambled to look for them. They had no luck and it wasn't until the late afternoon the third day that a French torpedo boat spotted the aircraft and its crew tossing about on the rough seas some fifty miles from land. They had run out of fuel after misjudging the length of time they had been in the air and had to touch down on the water and ride out the bad weather. The following report is now part of US Naval History:

Thursday, Nov. 22, 1917.
Weather conditions were not ideal for flying, clouds being very low and quite a sea running.

After leaving Le Croisic, we started south steering course 195. On reaching Île d'Yeu, found our drift to be considerably to the East. After picking up Pont Breton on Île d'Yeu, we sighted a four-masted bark, in ballast with auxiliary engine, to the N.E. We circled over her a number of times, increasing our radius on each turn until we were nearly out of sight of Île d'Yeu. We then left the bark and headed for Île d'Yeu. After searching the shore for mines and submarines, returned to Point Breton.

From Pt. Breton we steered course 29 for 45 minutes. We then headed due East for 30 minutes at altitude 50 metres. Motor died and we were forced to make a tail-to-wind landing. We found it possible to land the Tellier in rough water.

Dispatched at 2:30 p.m. pigeon with the following message:

> *Left Île d'Yeu at 1:10 p.m., headed 29 for 41 minutes. Then direct East 30min. had to come down, big sea running. Send all aid…*

Could not tell for certain our location. We took watches during the night. One bailed while the other two slept. As we could not get motor started, we thought over all possible things that could happen to it. Wilkinson had found that left gas tank had not been feeding; but too late to fix it as we could not see. Passed a very uncertain night. We knew they would do all possible things to help us.

Friday, Nov. 23, 1917.
Sent pigeon at 7:40 a.m. and message as follows:

> *Sighted last night two lighthouses on starboard bow which we considered Île d'Yeu. Send torpedo boats and aeroplanes. Have no food. We are taking in water. We are not positive of our location, but are going to sea. Send help. If you do not find us, say we died game to the end.*

Put in new spark plug, cleaned magneto, shifted gasoline from left to right tank. We were all so seasick that we could not work to best advantage. Bailed water out of boat. Wilkinson finally got motor started at 11:40 a.m. Saw hydroplane and blimp to the North of us. Did not give up hope. Beautiful day. Got motor going and started to taxi toward Île d'Yeu. We were not making much headway on account of the sea. Our left pontoon had filled with water. Finally decided our only hope was to try and get machine off water. As a result of trying, I broke left wing and got ourselves into a hell of a shape. Things began to look black. There was no founding fault with anyone. Couldn't help marvelling at the morale of the men. It was a case of heroic bravery on their part to see their only hope smashed.

We took part during the night, first lying on wing, then bailing, then sleeping. Wilkinson turned to and got all ready to cast adrift the left wing. We all decided to die game to the end…

An FBA flying boat with bombs beneath the wings and attached to the fuselage.

Wing began to crumble. We all decided to let it stay on as long as possible. Sea began to grow bitter toward evening, and the water began to come in. We all hoped that we would be able to ride out the night. Very uncomfortable night and we were all growing very weak. Very long night. Our hopes were beginning to go very low, but no one showed it.

Saturday Nov. 24, 1917.

Day finally came. Wing getting near to boat as it crumpled. It was heart-rending. We had to bail and stay out on wing-tip. As waves came over, we began to feel lower and lower. It was finally decided to cast off wing, and let what might come. We tried to get other wing ready to cast off, but we could not get off nuts as we were so weak and tools were inadequate. We were going over gradually on starboard side. We were all on port side trying to keep her righted. We then saw that there was no way of us staying up much longer unless we could get the wing off. We had just about given up everything when Wilkinson let out a yell that something was in sight. We were not able to believe our eyes. We thought it was a submarine, but we did not care. If it was a submarine, we hoped it would blow us up and end it all.

As luck would have it, the vessel was a French torpedo boat, who pulled alongside the battered wreck of the aircraft and hauled the three crew members to safety. The torpedo boat sank the battered Tellier flying boat with gunfire and took the American naval airmen back to hospital in La Pallice. Their first taste of wartime action nearly turned out to be their last, but what it did highlight was all aircraft had to equipped for every emergency and signalling devices, rations and sea anchors were a must.

Another incident at NAS Le Croisic on 4 March 1918, was nearly the last for two US Navy aviators, Joseph Cline and Frederick Lovejoy. As Joseph Cline lifted the flying boat off the water at Le Croisic, the bomb under the port wing fell off and exploded on contact with the water. The explosion almost simultaneously set off the other bomb under the starboard wing, the blast cutting the flying boat in half just behind the cockpit. The rear of the aircraft crashed in pieces back on to the water, whilst the front section fortunately remained almost intact and slid back onto the water. Neither man was hurt. Joseph Cline was later posted to NAS Brest, where he served with distinction until the Armistice.

The first attack on a German submarine by a US Naval aircraft took place on 25 March 1918, when Ensign John F. McNamara, flying from the NAS Portland, Dorset, attacked a submarine while it was on the surface. It had disappeared below the surface by the time McNamara had turned for another attack and he was given a 'probably damaged' evaluation. Later in October McNamara was posted to NAS Wexford, southern Ireland, where he again attacked a German submarine, this time causing severe damage but still not confirmed as a 'kill'.

On 27 April 1918, one of the Navy's first major successes of the war took place. Ensign Kenneth Smith and his observer QM/1c C.E. Williams were on patrol from NAS Île Tudy, near Brest, with another flying boat flown by R.H. Harrell, QM1c(A) and H.W. Struder, QM2c(A), when they spotted the periscope of a German submarine cruising just below the surface of the sea some distance from an incoming convoy. Calling for back-up from a couple of French torpedo-boats, Ensign Smith attacked the submarine with his bombs, scoring a direct hit. The French torpedo-boats also opened fire and between them they sank the submarine with all hands. For their part in the operation, the two American aviators were awarded the *Croix de Guerre* with Palm.

By the middle of 1918, the US Navy had a number of patrol aircraft operating from various French bases around the coast, they were at Le Croisic, Brest, L'Aber Vrach and Paimbœuf. In addition to these they had four seaplane patrol bases and one kite balloon base in Ireland at Queenstown, Wexford, Whiddy Island, Lough Foyle and Berehaven. The station at Berehaven on the southern tip of Ireland, was the base for kite balloons, thus enabling the convoys arriving from across the Atlantic to be afforded some degree of protection. With command of NAS Killingholme in their hands, the US Navy, together with their Allies, virtually controlled the area of sea between the North Sea and the Channel Islands. The lighter-than-air (LTA) operations of the First World War were overshadowed by the fighter and bomber exploits, but they played an important part in the patrols over the Atlantic approaches.

The sites for the US Naval bases had been chosen by the Admiralty in England and construction work on these bases started by T.J. Moran & Co. the British Admiralty contractors. With the arrival of the US Navy and the subsequent handing over of the bases to them, the US Navy then completed the construction. The need for a supply base close to the port of Dublin gave rise to the urgent selection of a site. The one chosen was a dilapidated warehouse with no roof or floor, 100ft wide and 390ft long, at 76 Sir John Rogerson's Quay in Dublin. It became known as the United States Naval Aviation Supply Base and stored its first materials there in March 1918.

Queenstown became the first NAS in Ireland and was located close to the village of Aghada. On 14 February 1918, it became the headquarters of Cdr F. McCrary, Commander US Naval Air Stations, Ireland, although the naval air station itself was under the command of LCDR Paul J. Peyton. All aircraft that arrived in Dublin in crates were shipped to Queenstown by road for assembly and testing before delivery to their respective air stations. It was also an ideal training base for air crews, as they would be close enough to the war zone without actually being in it. They could be trained to carry out patrols over the Western Approaches, without the risk of being attacked by enemy aircraft.

The construction of the base was a source of concern for the Navy, who employed their own labour force from the local inhabitants, only to find that the necessary equipment was not available. A large, very old and dilapidated steam shovel was found in an abandoned quarry and after much bargaining with its owner, it was dismantled, loaded on to lorries and transported to the site of the base. After a great deal of repair work it was ready, and managed to complete all its excavation tasks before finally giving up the ghost. After what must have seemed like an eternity, the base was ready to receive its first aircraft. The first eight seaplanes arrived at Queenstown harbour aboard the USS *Cuyama* of 27 June 1918. From the ship they were placed aboard lighters and ferried to NAS Queenstown. It is said that it took longer to ferry the aircraft from the ship to the naval air station, than it did to bring them from the United States to Queenstown harbour. A further ten more aircraft arrived on 24 July aboard the USS *Kanawha*, and by the end of the war this number had risen to thirty-eight.

It wasn't until the end of August that the first of the seaplanes took to the air to carry out any kind of patrol and it wasn't until October that the first contact with the enemy was made. During this month, over forty patrols were flown accounting for over 130 hours flying time.

As the size of the US Naval force grew in Ireland, an additional US naval air station was set up at Ferrybank in Wexford harbour and was known as NAS Wexford. Construction work by the British Admiralty had started back in December 1917 and it was formally handed over to the US Navy on 2 May 1918. It was commanded by LCDR Herbster and consisted of two hangars and a variety of other buildings and amenities. Accommodation, unlike the other US Naval bases in Ireland, was quite luxurious. Two mansion houses, Bann Aboo and Ely House, were taken over and renovated and then, after the enlisted men's quarters had been built, turned into the officers' mess.

From NAS Wexford, patrols covered the southern entrance to the Irish Sea, east of Queenstown and just twelve miles from the Tuskar Rock lighthouse. It was the busiest area for shipping traffic, as most of the shipping in and out of the United Kingdom passed through its waters. Consequently it also became the hunting ground for German submarines, and air patrols had to be extremely vigilant when convoys were due in the area. At the same time as NAS Wexford was being activated, another naval air station, NAS Lough Foyle, this time on the remote northern tip of Ireland, was being constructed. Its location, although ideally placed for a patrol squadron, caused numerous problems for the construction gangs. All materials had to be shipped by sea up to Londonderry and then by road to the site (later, aircraft destined for Lough Foyle, were assembled at NAS Queenstown, and flown around the coast to the base using NAS Wexford as a transient base). It wasn't until 31 July 1918 that the naval air station was completed and ready for operational use. The purchase of a 24ft whaleboat and two dinghies so that the crews and supplies could be ferried out to the moored seaplanes, completed the itinerancy for the base. All they wanted now were the seaplanes.

Just prior to the opening of the base, a ship from the United States carrying five seaplanes destined for the base, sailed past to the cheers and waves of the air and ground crews who were waiting for the aircraft to arrive.

Although the seaplanes based in Ireland never had any success in real terms, their presence caused the German Naval High Command to become extremely wary. It is an accepted fact that the waters around these patrol area became among the safest for Allied shipping and not a safe place for the 'Kaiser's tin fish', as one American war correspondent put it.

The result of a premature bomb explosion in mid-air on an FBA flying boat.

The first American aircraft to arrive in France from the United States, were Curtiss HS-1 seaplanes with Liberty engines. They were assembled at Brest, then delivered to other American stations along the French coast. At first all the aircrews were excited with the prospect of getting into the air and joining in the fight, then it was discovered that when they had built the aircraft, the manufacturers had not taken into consideration all the additional equipment that would be necessary to turn the aircraft into a war machine. By the time bombs, machine-guns, radios, aldis lamps, fire extinguishers, pigeons and enough fuel for a four hour patrol were installed, the aircraft could not get off the water. Another six feet had to be added to the wing span and the aircraft was re-designated the HS-2. Even then, three strands of salmson cord had to be installed on the right rudder to offset the torque, in order to fly the aircraft normally.

The US Navy had also established a base in Italy, at Porto Corsini, fifty miles south of Venice on the shores of the Adriatic Sea. It was under the command of Lt Willis B. Haviland, but under the direct control of the Italian Director of Marine Aviation. The site of the base at Porto Corsini was at the V-junction of two canals that opened out into the Adriatic Sea, and had been determined because of its location in relation to the Austrian base of Pola on the other side of the Adriatic Sea. The battleships and cruisers of the Austrian High Seas Fleet were anchored at Pola and it was one of the main bases for the German and Austrian submarines that hunted in the Mediterranean.

The US Navy's arrival at Porto Corsini was recognised by the Austrians by their carrying out an attack on the base – but they were unable to inflict any damage or casualties.

Initially it was thought that there might be a language barrier between the Americans and the Italians, but fortunately the US Navy had pre-empted this problem and with Lt Haviland they had sent Naval Aviator Bosun (T) Giochini Varini. Varini had been born in Venice and had emigrated to San Francisco as a young man. The fact that he spoke both English and Italian fluently and was fully versed in the local customs and ways made the transition and integration of the 300 American Navy men into the community a relatively easy one.

At first there were problems in getting the Italians to actually fight the Austrians – they seemed to be content in just carrying out observation flights and dropping leaflets. Because the US Navy was directly under the control of the Director of Marine Aviation, the Americans had went along with it in the beginning. But as time progressed they explored the enemy coastline in greater depth and eventually were able to persuade the Director to allow them to carry out bombing raids on the Austrians bases. At first it was decided to operate HS-2Ls and Macchi 5s from the base, but the wingspan of the HS-2L was far too wide for the canals and the Macchis were only just manageable with great caution. It was decided to use the M-8 seaplane whose wingspan was just under the width of the canal, but only very limited bomb loads could be carried. Training was carried out on Lake Bolsena on an area, marked off by buoys, which equalled the width of the Porto Corsini canals. Within a few weeks the pilots had mastered the take offs and landings sufficiently enough to enable the Macchi 5s to be re-introduced.

One of the first contacts with the enemy was on 21 August 1918, when a flight of bombers and fighters from NAS Porto Corsini, en route to attack the Austrian base at Pola on the other side of the Adriatic Sea, was attacked by a force of Austrian fighters over the Austrian naval base there. During the ensuing fight one of the American aircraft was shot down by Fregattenleutnant Stephan Wolleman, flying a Pheonix D.I fighter, just three miles from the entrance to the harbour at Pola. The pilot, Ensign George Ludlow, managed to get his badly

An excellent shot of USNAS Porto Corsini taken from the air showing the extremely narrow canal that had to be used for take-offs and landings.

damaged Macchi M.5 seaplane onto the water. Ensign Charles Hammann, even though his own aircraft had been damaged, followed him down and landed alongside Ludlow's now sinking aircraft. Even though he was under constant bombardment from the shore batteries at Pola, Hammann kept his engine running whilst Ludlow swam to him. As he clambered on to the fuselage of Hammann's aircraft, it was realised that the only place for Ludlow was lying beneath the engine atop the fuselage and hanging on to the engine struts. Hammann took off and safely returned to base. On landing on the canal at Porto Corsini, Hammann's Macchi, which had been damaged during the rescue, flipped over on to its back on landing. It was Ludlow this time who was to rescue Hammann, who was trapped by his safety belt. For the heroic rescue off Pola, Hammann received the Medal of Honour – albeit posthumously – and the Italian Silver Medal of Valour, whilst Ludlow received the Navy Cross and the Italian Bronze Medal of Valour. Less than a year later Ensign Hammann lost his life in a crash in a Macchi M.5 seaplane. It was only then that he was awarded the Medal of Honour for the rescue of Ludlow.

The following night the Austro-Hungarians retaliated and ten aircraft from Pola attacked the USN base at Porto Corsini. They dropped a total of forty-nine bombs, only one of which hit the base itself, the remainder exploding harmlessly in the canal. The following night the Americans attacked Pola with greater success than the Austro-Hungarians. They damaged the port's defences and aircraft hangars. There were one or two small skirmishes on 24 and 29 August 1918, but nothing major.

A reconnaissance flight by six Macchi M-5s on 7 October proved to the Americans that Pola's defences were very weak. The US Naval aircraft left Porto Corsini at 0700 hours and returned at 0900 hours, after circling the Austro-Hungarian base twice and being subjected to sporadic and inaccurate anti-aircraft fire. At one point five enemy aircraft were seen to take off to intercept them, but declined to engage them. This just reinforced the Americans' opinion that the Austria-Hungary was a beaten nation.

The last significant attack by the Americans on Pola was on 22 October 1918, when eight Macchi M-5s, three Macchi M-8s and two FBAs from Porto Corsini joined with thirty naval aircraft from an Italian squadron based in Venice. The attack was a complete success and all the aircraft returned unharmed. The Austro-Hungarians had virtually nothing left with which to retaliate and at the end of October all raids ceased. The following month the war was over.

The US Navy in Italy achieved little in this part of the world with regard to the war effort – this was not their fault, however, but more that of the Italian High Command's unwillingness to fight. The only American casualty of the air war concerning Porto Corsini had been when Ensign Louie J. Bergen crashed whilst landing his Macchi M.5 on the canal.

In France, four sites were selected for the combined US Navy and Marine bomber squadrons, the US Navy squadrons 1, 2, 3, and 4 would use the bases at St Inglevert and Campagne and the US Marine squadrons A, B. C and D, commanded by Lts Geiger, McIlvain, Capt. Douglas Roben and 1st Lt Russell A. Presley respectively, would use Oye and LaFresne. The only aircraft available at the time were a few DH-9s and 4s that had come from the RAF. In America, production of the DH-4 bomber was still going on and a reception base for these aircraft was required in France, prior to them being sent to the Navy and Marine Corps bases.

One of the bases set up in June 1918 by Lt Kenneth Whiting, USN, was at Dunkirk, which combined squadrons of the US Marine Corps and Navy. These were collectively known as the Northern Bombing Group and first flew under the command of Capt. David C. Hanrahan, USN, in February 1918, with Caproni aircraft supplied by the army. The group was originally planned to operate a day wing and a night wing from the Calais-Dunkirk area, and consisted of six squadrons in each wing. Within the vicinity of this group was an assembly, repair and supply unit known as Base B. The operational project of the group initially, was to continuously bomb German submarine bases at Ostend, Zeebrugge and Bruges. On 31 May 1918, a

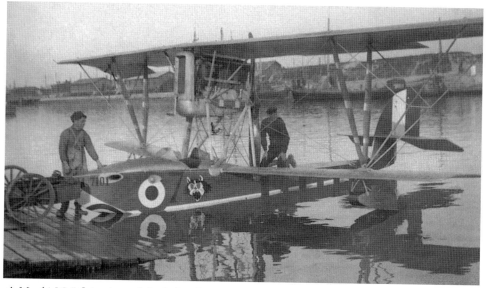

A Macchi M.5 flying boat of the Italian Navy at USNAS Porto Corsini.

The complement of officers of the United States Naval Air Service base at Porto Corsini.

cable was received from the Department of the Navy stating that the group be reduced to four squadrons in each wing. One month later another cable cast doubts about having such a base in Northern France, because of the military situation at the time. It was decided to secure a site in Southern England and the British Air Ministry was approached. Late in July 1918, it was decided to turn over the existing base at Eastleigh, near Southampton, over to the US Navy under the command of Lt Geoffrey de Chevalier, USN. The flying time from Eastleigh to France was only 1½ hours, and enabled all materials transported across the Atlantic to be unloaded at the major port of Southampton which was only a few miles away from Eastleigh.

The new location of Base B caused the airfields of the bomber squadrons in France, to be moved correspondingly. Night Squadrons 1 and 2 moved to St Inglevert; 3 and 4 to Campagne; Day Squadrons 7 and 8 to Oye and 9 and 10 to Le Frene. The headquarters of the group was also moved to Antingues, just outside Ardres.

At the end of July 1918, the first United States Marine Corps pilots together with their ground crews and equipment, arrived at Brest, France, en route to their base at Calais. Earlier in the year one of their number had visited France to inspect the French and Italian bomber bases. He was Marine Corps Aviator No.1 Maj. Arthur Cunningham, USMC, and his primary job was to select bases for the combined Northern Bomber Group pilots who were to follow him from the United States. His main problem was that he had more than enough pilots to fill the squadrons, but the NBG (Northern Bomber Group) had no aircraft. Cunningham had had earlier problems with the US Army, who had told him quite bluntly that they wanted nothing to do with him or his pilots. He had persuaded the General Board of the Navy that his Marine pilots could bomb the German submarine bases, therefore releasing the US Navy aircraft to carry out other duties. The Navy Board approved the setting up of a so-called Northern Bombing Group and Cunningham set about joining up all the other Marine units into the 1st Marine Aviation Force. The aircraft he had been offered was the Italian Caproni 600, but Cunningham had wanted the Caproni 450 with the Isotta-Fraschini engine. The Caproni 600 had the Italian Fiat engines and had been proved to be most unreliable and in some cases downright dangerous.

Hundreds of the Caproni 600 were ordered by the United States but only a handful were ever delivered and the ones that did arrive were plagued with problems of poor quality workmanship and engine malfunctions. It was said that the Caproni 600 with the Fiat engine killed more Allied crews than the Germans and Austrians combined.

It has to be remembered that nearly all the American aviators were still in the learning stage of combat and that a large number of them had been assigned to battle-hardened Allied units. These pilots were to become a major asset to the main force of the USAS and USNAS when they finally arrived, and before the war was over the American pilots and their squadrons would leave their mark on the world of military aviation.

At the beginning of June 1918, a number of US Navy pilots and observers were assigned to No.214 Squadron, RAF, at St Inglevert, for combat training on Handley-Page bombers after their base at Coudekerque had been bombed. By the middle of July the US Navy crews had enough training and experience to go on raids manned entirely by American crews. The first of the long-awaited Caproni bombers arrived on 11 August 1918. Four days later, flown by Ensigns Leslie Taber and Charles Fahy with D.C. Hale as gunner/observer, they made a successful night raid on the submarine pens in Ostend. But this was marred by two more missions that had to be aborted because of engine trouble. More time was spent in repairing and trying, most of the time unsuccessfully, to keep these aircraft serviceable. The only combat time the American crews were able to get was with No. 214 Squadron on their Handley-Page bombers.

After a couple of months of trying to make the Caproni an acceptable bomber, an arrangement was made between the US Army and British authorities to procure British Handley-Page bombers in exchange for Liberty engines; the latter were to be mounted in the Handley-Page aircraft. The agreement was reached but the night-bombers were only just being tested as hostilities ceased.

The funeral procession of two US Naval aviators at Porto Corsini.

Macchi M.5 flying boat making a landing on the canal at NAS Porto Corsini.

One pilot, Lt (jg) McCormick, USNRF, had carried a number of flights at night and was assigned to 214 Squadron RAF, to fly bombing missions in the Handley-Page. Returning from a bombing mission in the middle of the night, and having suffered flak damage, the aircraft crashed in a forced landing. McCormick managed to extricate himself from the wreckage and then ran forward to aid the RAF members of the crew. In the darkness he ran into one of the large propellers that was still turning and was killed.

The Marine/Navy day-bomber squadrons had more success, however, when they were given DH-4 bombers with Liberty engines. Four of the aircraft were shipped over from the United States and assembled at Pauillac. After being assembled they were inspected by American and British engineers, and after a number of modifications were put into active service. More of the aircraft were expected from the United States, but after a number of delays, the Commander, US Naval Aviation Forces, Foreign Service, obtained by concession of the British government, 54 DH-9 aircraft in exchange for Liberty engines. These aircraft were assembled at Eastleigh and flown across the English Channel to Pauillac, before being assigned to their various squadrons. The first aircraft arrived on the 2 October 1918, just too late to make any significant impact on the war. The day wing of the NBG was flown by the US Marines but, like their Navy counterparts, they were lacking in combat experience. Three crews were assigned to No.218 Squadron, RAF, for 'hands-on' combat training and after qualifying returned to their own units. This system proved to be extremely successful, so the American crews were rotated so that at any one time there was a pool of US Navy and Marine pilots and observers being trained by the RAF.

The Marine crews did, however, manage to get involved in operations. Because of a shortage of pilots, the RAF, who had taken a battering over the war years, had more aircraft than crews. An arrangement was made with the two RAF squadrons, Nos 217 and 218, for the US Marines to fly three bombing missions with them, it was one that gained approval from both sides. On 28 September 1918 whilst flying with 218 Squadron, RAF, the US Marines scored their first victory, when 1st Lt E.S. Brewster and Gy (Gunnery) Sgt H.B. Wersheiner, although both wounded when attacked by fighters over Belgium, shot down a German Albatros. A week later three Marine crews, again operating with 218 Squadron,

RAF, were involved in a dramatic relief operation. The crews, consisting of Lt Frank Nelms and Gy Sgt Archie Pascal, Capt. R.S. Lytle and Gy Sgt A. Winman and Capt. F.P. Mulcahy and Gy Sgt T.L. McCullough, dropped over 2,600lb of food and supplies to a beleaguered French regiment, who were cut off from the main supply lines. For carrying out this dangerous mercy mission, the pilots were awarded the Distinguished Service Cross (DSC), whilst the Gy Sgts were awarded the Navy Cross.

The 1st Marine Aviation Force, as it was then known, was brought up to strength with 149 officers and 842 enlisted men. Maj. Cunningham's original plan to bomb the German submarine pens was shelved because the retreating Germans had evacuated them all. This enabled the Marine squadrons, now renumbered 7, 8, 9, and 10, to operate alongside their RAF counterparts in support of the British and Belgian ground forces who were gathering momentum in the final push.

At 1100 hours on 11 November 1918, the war in Europe ended and an Armistice was declared. Although the USAS, USNAS and the USMCAS had entered the war only in the last fifteen months, their contribution was more than enough to tip the balance in favour of the Allies.

United States Naval Aircraft of the First World War

Curtiss 'America'	FBA flying boat
Curtiss H.8	
Curtiss H.12	Macchi M-3 flying boat
Curtiss 'Large America'	Macchi M-5 flying boat
Curtiss R.2	Macchi M-8 flying boat

A Macchi M.5 on the slipway at NAS Porto Corsini.

7
French Naval Air Service

The French Naval Air Service had its beginnings in 1910, with the creation of an aviation division. The air service was divided into two sections, a lighter-than-air (airships and dirigibles) and aircraft, the latter becoming the more dominant after the outbreak of the First World War. The former torpedo-boat carrier *Foudre* was converted in 1912 to become a seaplane carrier and equipped to carry between four and eight seaplanes, mostly Voisins or Caudrons. She was also the first warship to have an aircraft hangar fitted on to her deck, just aft of her third funnel. The *Foudre* originally had a platform installed over her forecastle with the intention of using it to launch aircraft, and, on 8 May 1914, civilian Ren Caudron flying one of his own designed aircraft, the Caudron G.III amphibian floatplane, carried out the first take-off from a French ship. One month later a second attempt carried out by one of France's first qualified military pilots, Lt de Vaissaeau Jean de Laborde, ended when he crashed into the sea just after taking off. At the beginning of the First World War, the *Foudre* was attached to the Arme Navale in the Mediterranean and equipped with Nieuport floatplanes that had originally been ordered by the Turkish government.

During the Gallipoli-Dardanelles campaign, aircraft from the *Foudre* carried out a number of reconnaissance flights, but they were not equipped with wireless so their use was limited. In August 1915 her Nieuport floatplanes were replaced by FBA flying boats but carried out few aviation duties for the rest of the war. She was one of the few seaplane-carriers that remained on duty after the war; she was scrapped in 1922.

Like Britain, France had a very large coastline and subsequently developed a number of coastal installations for anti-submarine and reconnaissance operations. The first of these stations were at Fréjus and Saint-Raphaël. These stations were equipped with a variety of aircraft at the beginning of the war. Among the twenty-five aircraft available to the Aviation Maritime, were thirteen Nieuport 6H/M monoplanes, three Caudrons, one Breguet and eight different types of Voisins. Of the thirteen Nieuports, appropriated from a Turkish order at the manufacturers, seven were based at Saint-Raphaël, the remainder at Hourtin and Bizerte.

Navy pilots were trained initially at army flying schools, then sent to either Saint Raphaël, Hourtin or Bizerte for advanced training. Observers were trained by naval instructors at Saint-Raphaël and gunners were trained at Cazeaux by army instructors.

The first two main centres, or *centres d'aviation*, for French Maritime Aviation were at Boulogne and Dunkirk and were set up in December 1914. Their initial role was for anti-submarine duties, but it was soon realised that they could be used for raids against the German submarine bases at Zeebrugge and Ostende. At the beginning of January 1915, five bombers were delivered to Boulogne, two Voisin 3s, one Breguet, one Farman and one FBA. They were equipped to carry only 2-4kg bombs, but trials were carried out using 10kg bombs with delayed fuses. This allowed the bombs to enter the water to a depth of 6m before exploding.

The first of these raids was carried out on 4 February 1915, the aircraft being sent out individually. The mission proved to be totally ineffective and it became obvious that, to make any impact at all, the aircraft would have to be sent out in groups. By the end of the month the aircraft at Dunkirk had been reinforced with FBA Type B flying boats and a number of land-based Voisins. Requests were made to the Aviation Militaire by the Aviation Maritime for the new Morane-Saulniers and Nieuports, but they were refused and were told they would have to make the best of what they had. It was decided to use the now outdated Voisins for bombing raids and during the following three months, they carried out thirty-five raids, dropping 552 bombs on the submarine bases at Zeebrugge and Ostende. Trials had been carried out using the FBA flying boats on the raids, but their inability to climb above 6,000ft with a full bomb load, which was very limited in any case, left them extremely vulnerable to anti-aircraft fire. It was quite obvious that a much larger aircraft, with a greater bomb-load carrying capability and a greater range, was required for long-range bombing and reconnaissance missions.

The main problem of aircraft assigned to the Aviation Maritime, was that none had been designed for use on or over water. They were land-based aircraft, so a number of modifications had to be made before they were suitable for use by the French Naval Air Service, i.e. floats to replace the wheels, flotation bags inside the aircraft in case of ditching. These renovations were not helped by the ever-changing command structure, which caused no end of problems whenever new reconnaissance techniques, equipment and general strategies were implemented.

In March 1915 the navy received the first of its airships when two S.S.Zs and a C-class airship arrived from Britain. By 1916 the navy had opened bases all along the channel coast equipping them with Astra-Torres, Chalais-Meudon and Zodiac airships. The following year the army transferred control of their airships to the navy, which enabled the navy to extend its theatre of operations to the Mediterranean. Bases were opened up in Salonika, Algiers, Corfu, Oran and Bizerte and all were equipped with twin-engined dirigibles armed with machine guns and 75mm guns.

To train the crews for this rapidly expanding part of the French Naval Air Service, a school was set up at Rochefort-sur-Mer. The success of the school can be measured quite accurately, when it is an indisputable fact that no convoy accompanied by these airships, was ever attacked by submarine. Their record of successes against submarines spotted by these airships is not so good, however, as only four were ever said to have been destroyed. However they did the job they were required to do, i.e. escort duties and reconnaissance flights, without fault.

The airship Astra-Torres 4.

By December 1915 the Centre de Aviation, as it was now known, had established three bases in France (Dunkirk, Boulogne and Le Havre), one in Brindisi, Italy, and one in Salonika, Greece. The latter two bases were used to carry out reconnaissance patrols over the Adriatic and the Mediterranean. One *escadrille*, flying Nieuports, was sent to Egypt where it operated out of Port Said. Two German merchant ships, the SS *Aenne Rickmers* and the SS *Rabenfels*, had been seized whilst in harbour there during 1914 and were converted to seaplane carriers. These two German ships served in the Mediterranean and Red Sea throughout the war, alongside a former French liner, the *Campinas* and a former British cross-channel ship the *Rouen*. The two German ships were later renamed HMS *Anne* and HMS *Raven II*, and commissioned into service with the Royal Navy.

The *Campinas*, owned by the Chargeurs Reunis cargo liner company, was requisitioned by the French authorities at Port Said at the end of 1915 and converted to a seaplane carrier by the Compagnie Universelle du Canal de Suez. In reality the word 'conversion' is misleading, because all that was actually done was to install canvas aircraft hangars fore and aft. Her complement of aircraft consisted of six Nieuport floatplanes initially, which were replaced one year later by six FBA seaplanes.

Operating in the eastern Mediterranean-Aegean-Levant areas throughout the remainder of the war, the *Campinas* led a relatively quiet existence and had an undistinguished operational life. Her whereabouts after the war are not known, but it is believed she was returned to her owners.

In June 1915, an *escadrille* of FBAs was stationed in Venice. The idea was to carry out reconnaissance flights along the Austrian coastline and later bombing raids. The idea was good in principle but disastrous in practice. For over two years the *escadrille*, understaffed and ill-equipped, carried out reconnaissance flights and bombing missions over Trieste, Parenzo, Miramare and Citta Nuova and even though their aircraft were being continually upgraded, they were no match for the Austrian flying boats. The *escadrille* suffered tremendous losses during this period and it is indicative of the dangers the pilots and observers faced at this time, for when it was disbanded in 1917, not one of the original officers had survived.

The base at Brindisi was used for anti-submarine and reconnaissance patrols in the Adriatic and Mediterranean and also for bombing raids against the Turkish arsenal at Pola. Initially a temporary base at Gardo had been established, to enable the FBAs to carry out raids against Pola. But after one particularly savage return raid by the Austrians, it was decided to withdraw the surviving FBAs to Brindisi. An *escadrille* of Nieuport 6Hs based there discovered, in December 1915, that Turkish troops were using the road from Hedjaz to Maan to reinforce their bases at Adana and Ber-Saba. A number of attacks were then carried out on the road, the railway lines and the camps themselves causing a great deal of damage. By early 1916, the British had created their own air service and took over the role in that area. The Nieuports were then sent to Port Said to help the British protect the Suez Canal, finally being disbanded in April 1916.

The *Foudre* continued to patrol the Mediterranean, the only vessel capable of carrying aircraft and have the on-board facilities to maintain and repair them. This was to be of paramount importance at a later date, when the *Foudre* took part in Dardanelles Campaign. Her two-seat Nieuport float aircraft, on the other hand, were of little use as spotter aircraft in the campaign because of their lack of wireless equipment.

In France the war raged on and the sizes of the various *escadrilles* increased markedly enabling more and larger bombing missions to be carried out against the German bases.

By the end of 1916, the Aviation Maritime had established itself around Europe and the Middle East. They had *centres d'aviation* in France – Dunkirk, Boulogne, Le Havre, La Pallice and Toulon; in Greece – Salonika, Corfu and Argostoli; and in North Africa – Bizerte; and also a *poste de combat* at Bône.

The beginning of 1917 brought marine aviation into its own. The German submarine menace was causing chaos to the merchant ships that struggled to bring much-needed supplies to the allies. It was decided that the only way to combat the situation, was to dramatically increase the size and strength of the Aviation Maritime. The organisation was developed into three districts:

1. The patrol of the English Channel and North Sea
2. Patrol of the Atlantic Ocean and English Channel
3. Patrol of the Mediterranean

The No.1 district was split into two zones – a & b:

(a) known as Aviation Maritime in the GAN Zone, was under the command of Lt de Vaisseau Lofevre and had two *escadrilles* consisting of thirty-two aircraft, twelve at Dunkirk and twelve at Saint-Pol. The remaining eight were held in reserve.

(b) Aviation Maritime – English Channel was commanded by Lt de Vaisseau Serre and had twenty-two aircraft, sixteen at the *centre de* Boulogne and six at *poste de combat de* Dieppe. Dieppe was also the centre for the *escadrille côtière* (coastal) *de* Eu and *centre de dirigeables de* Marquise-Rinxent – commanded by Lt de Vaisseau Larrouy.

The No.2 district, Patrol of the Atlantic Ocean and the English Channel, was split into three sections:

(a) The 1st Division at Normandy.
(b) The 2nd Division for Brittany
(c) The 3rd Division for Gascony and Biscay.

The (a) section, the 1st Division for Normandy, had its centre at Le Havre, commanded by Lt de Vaisseau Flamanc and had sixteen FBAs. There was a *poste de combat* at Cherbourg, equipped with twenty-four aircraft, an *escadrille conoitre de* Lion-sur-Mer under the command of Capitaine Lafay whose prime mission was to patrol the Ouistreham area for submarines

The crew car of the airship Alsace.

and mines. The *centre de* Guernsey, under the command of Lt de Vaisseau Le Cours Grand-Maison, was equipped with twelve seaplanes – Telliers and FBAs.

On 31 January 1918 two seaplanes from Guernsey attacked a German submarine – severely damaging it. The seaplanes were in action again on 23 April when they attacked a submarine seen cruising on the surface. Releasing a homing pigeon, the crew of the aircraft requested another seaplane to continue the attack as they had run out of bombs. A third aircraft was duly dispatched and the submarine, believing it was safe, was bombed and sunk. On 31 May an English sailing ship was attacked by a German submarine as it started down through the Channel. Two seaplanes from Guernsey on patrol spotted that attack and drove off the submarine with bombs. Later the same day another submarine was attacked by aircraft from the same base. It is not recorded whether or not the submarines were sunk. These sorties proved that the English Channel was not the safe hunting ground for submarines as was first thought.

On 13 September 1918 two seaplanes from Lion-sur-Mer, who were escorting a convoy, saw and attacked a German submarine as it was about to attack one of the ships in the convoy. They dropped two bombs, forcing the submarine to dive. It never surfaced again, so it is not known if it was damaged or not. There were no attacks on the convoy for the rest of the trip.

There were also two *centres des dirigeables*, one at Le Havre, the other at Montebourg. On 12 March 1918, the French airship AT-O, commanded by Lt Sainte Rémy, was flying out of Le Havre when it saw an enemy submarine on the surface and attacked it with bombs. Rémy claimed that the submarine fired upon him as he approached, and he then returned fire with machine guns and bombs and sunk it. Unfortunately the 'enemy' submarine turned out to be the British submarine D-3, commanded by Lt W. Maitland-Dougall of the Royal Canadian Navy, which sank with the loss of all hands. A Board of Enquiry subsequently found that it was the lack of communication and failed identification of inter-Allied recognition signals that was the major factor in the accident.

The crew of an airship on escort patrol communicating with a warship.

The airship Adjutant Vincenot.

The (b) section, 2nd Division for Brittany, had as its main base the *centre de* Lorient commanded by Lt de Vaisseau Destrem, and was equipped with sixteen seaplanes that were used to protect convoys and attack submarines. It also had a forward base, *poste de combat* Croisic, equipped with seaplanes. This base was handed over to the United States Naval Air Service (USNAS) on 27 November 1917. A second base was created in June 1917, the *centre de Tréguier*, but it too was handed over to the USNAS in November 1917, as was the *centre des dirigeables de* Paimbœuf at the beginning of 1918 and *poste de combat* Île Tudy in June 1917. There were three *escadrilles* attached to Brittany, *escadrille côtière de* Plomeur, *escadrille côtière de* Quiberon and *escadrille côtière de* La Baule.

The third section (c) for Gascony and Biscay, had two main bases, *centre de* La Pallice, commanded by Lt de Vaisseau Truzy and *centre de* Bayonne commanded by Lt de Vaisseau Vielhomme, with *postes de combat* at La Rochelle, Socoa, Cazeaux and Hourtin. These three *postes de combat* were served by two *escadrilles*, *escadrille côtière des* Sables d'Olonne commanded by Capitaine Thouvenin and *escadrille côtière du* Verdon commanded by Capitaine Fontaine. There was also the *centre des dirigeables* Rochefort commanded by Lt de Vaisseau Sable, equipped with seven airships.

The No. 3 district, Patrol of the Mediterranean had three main sections:

(a) 1st Division for Algeria
(b) 2nd Division for Provence
(c) 3rd Division for the central Mediterranean

The (a) section consisted of eleven bases, *centre de* Algiers was commanded by Enseigne de Vaisseau Le Vayer and had twenty-four seaplanes at its disposal. *Centre de Bizerte* (thirty-two aircraft), *centre de* Oran (twelve seaplanes), *centre de* Arzew (twelve seaplanes), centre de Bône (twelve seaplanes), *centre de* Sousse (sixteen seaplanes), *centre de* Marsala (sixteen seaplanes), *centre des dirigeables de* La Senia, *centre des dirigeables d'*Alger-Baraki and *centre des dirigeables* de Bizerte.

A CM airship of the French Navy, flying over the Chalais-Meudon Airship Depot.

The (b) section consisted of ten bases with their centre being *poste de combat* Toulon. *Centre de* Perpignan, under the command of Lt de Vaisseau Le Villain, had twelve seaplanes and covered the area between Barcelona and Saintes-Maries-de-la-Mer. *Centre de* Toulon, under the command of Capitane de Fregate Richard, had sixteen seaplanes and controlled the area from Marseille to Italy. The carried out convoy escort duties and mine searching. *Centre de* Séte was originally *poste de combat* Perpignan but was changed to a centre under the command of Lt de Vaisseau Roux. *Centre de* Antibes had ten seaplanes and was commanded by Lt de Vaisseau Val. *Centre d'*Ajaccio was equipped with sixteen seaplanes. *Centre de* Bastia – sixteen seaplanes. *Escadrille côtière de* Marseilles, which was commanded by Capitane Picheral, had sixteen seaplanes. *Centre de dirigeables* de Aubagne – ten seaplanes. *Centre de dirigeables de* Cuers Pierrefeu – six seaplanes. *Centre de dirigeables de* Mezzana – sixteen seaplanes, under the command of Lt de Vaisseau Jouglard.

The (c) section consisted of fifteen bases including a number of minor *postes de combat*. *Centre de* Corfu, commanded by Lt de Vaisseau Hautefeuille, was the largest of all the bases with thirty-six seaplanes: twenty-four Donnet-Denhauts and twelve Telliers, and four Sopwith $1\frac{1}{2}$ Strutter fighters. On 20 February 1918 a section from the base spotted a German submarine on the surface and attacked it with 22kg and 52kg bombs. The submarine dived during the attack and oil was seen later on the surface indicating that it had been damaged, but the sinking of the submarine was never confirmed. *Escadrille d'avions de chasse de* Potamos, commanded by Sous-Lt Philbert, was equipped with six Nieuport fighters. *Centre de montage de* Brindisi was used as an assembly area for aircraft designated for other bases. *Centre de* Salonika encompassed four *postes de combat*: Kassandra, Panomi, Skiatho and Sikia. *Escadrille du Campinas* was in fact the seaplane carrier *Campinas* which went from base to base, and whose aircraft protected convoys and carried out reconnaissance flights on enemy troop movements. It was three of the seaplanes from the *Campinas* that, whilst on a routine patrol on 13 May 1918, spotted a minefield near the Aegean island of Milos and guided the minesweepers *Morse* and *Rateau* to the area to remove them. *Centre de* Piraeus – eight FBA flying boats. *Centre de* Milos – sixteen seaplanes. *Escadrille côtière de* Panormos – six F.40 Farman seaplanes. *Escadrille côtière de* Kourtesis – twelve Caudron G.6s and *centre de* Milos – twenty FBA flying boats and two Tellier T.6s.

Initially all the naval aviation bases were set up for convoy duties and reconnaissance missions, but as the war progressed the crews became more confident and competent. The hunting of submarines increased with a noticeable degree of success as the number of successful attacks showed in their results. The air arm of the French Navy, although at first appearing to be a poor relative, showed that its contribution to the success of the war was invaluable in helping to prevent the Germans in securing control of the English Channel.

French Naval Aircraft of the First World War

Borel-Odier Torpedo Bomber
Breguet – Reconnaissance Aircraft
Caudron G.III Hydravion
Donnet Denhaut
Donnet-Denhaut – DD2 – Coastal Patrol Aircraft
Donnet-Denhaut – DD8 – Coastal Reconnaissance Aircraft
Donnet-Denhaut – DD9 – Coastal Reconnaissance Aircraft
Donnet Denhaut – DD10 – Coastal Reconnaissance Aircraft
FBA★-B – Coastal Patrol
FBA-C – Coastal Patrol/Trainer
FBA-H – Coastal Reconnaissance Aircraft
FBA-S – Coastal Reconnaissance Aircraft
Georges Levy HB-2 – Maritime Reconnaissance Aircraft
Maurice Farman Floatplane
Nieuport VI – Coastal and Shipboard aircraft
Tellier – Maritime Reconnaissance Aircraft
Paul Schmitt X – Patrol Aircraft
Voisin
★ FBA= Franco-British Aviation

A Tellier flying boat of the French Navy. One model of the aircraft was fitted with a 47mm cannon for hunting submarines.

8
Russian Naval Air Service

The Russian Navy started to take a serious interest in aviation in 1910, although they had shown a passing interest in the mid-1890s and had established a number 'aerostatic parks' on the Baltic. The idea of using balloons had come from Vice Admiral Stephan O. Makarov, a man of tremendous vision and one of the most able of all the Tsar's senior naval officers. By the beginning of the 1900s a number of balloon bases had been set up along the Black Sea and Baltic coasts. The first use of a balloon from a ship started at the beginning of 1904 with the converting of the steam cutter *Diomed*. The success of these trials prompted more from the armoured cruiser *Rossija* and a variety of other transports, using the balloon for air-to-sea communications, spotting for naval gunfire against shore targets, mine detecting and laying.

At the outbreak of the Russo-Japanese war, a wealthy former Russian naval officer purchased the former passenger liner *Lahn* and gave it to the Russian navy for conversion to a balloon ship. During May 1904, the armoured cruiser *Rossija* carried out thirteen successful ascents before the line broke on the fourteenth flight. The balloon was damaged beyond economical repair but had proved the usefulness of using balloons from ships for reconnaissance purposes.

Further experiments were carried out by an army engineer Capt. Fydor A. Postnikov, a graduate from the aeronautic school in St Petersburg, from a ship converted for balloon use – the *Kolyma*. In November 1904, under the watchful eye of Lt M.N. Bolshev, an expert in balloons and man-lifting kites, the conversion was carried out. The ship was renamed *Russ* and became the world's first true aviation ship; she was equipped with compression equipment, hydrogen generators and containers occupying three deck levels. Over 1,000m of telephone wire for air-to-ship communication was stowed aboard, together with cameras for aerial photography. In addition, four manned kite balloons were carried as smaller kite balloons for signalling purposes.

Unfortunately, all the hard work in converting this ex-liner was wasted. The years of sailing the Atlantic as a passenger liner had taken their toll on the engines and boilers, as well as the ship's structure. She had been destined to join the Third Pacific Fleet in March 1905, but was considered to be unseaworthy due to extensive rust in the boilers. Had she been at the Battle of Tsushima there is very little doubt that she would have not survived. The *Russ* was taken out of service the following year and sold as a merchantman. During the Second World War she was listed as an auxiliary in the Russian Fleet, but her fate is not known.

During the Battle of Tsushima another seaplane-carrier, the hybrid cruiser/yacht *Almaz*, served with the Second Pacific Squadron. Originally built as a vice-regal yacht for service in the Far East, the *Almaz* was the fastest of all the Black Sea Fleet seaplane carriers with a top speed of 19 knots. Capable of carrying three to four seaplanes, her aircraft were involved in operations in the Bosphorus, raids on Varna, Bulgaria and on the Turkish coast.

A large number of experiments had been carried out towing balloons and man-carrying kites from warships during the Russo-Japanese War showing that the balloon had a role to play in the field of reconnaissance and spotting for the big naval guns.

After the Russo-Japanese War there was an excess of two million roubles, 675,000 of which had been raised by public subscription. The Grand Duke Alexander Mikhailovich, a cousin of Tsar Nicholas II, who held naval flag rank, became fascinated by aviation when he heard about Louis Blériot's flight across the English Channel and decided to introduce aviation into Russia.

During the period when Grand Duke Alexander was visiting in France, he set about purchasing aircraft and arranging for selected officers to undergo flight training in France. The following year, Alexander purchased some land for a flight school to be established near Sebastapol in the Crimea. The site had been chosen because of its stable climate throughout most of the year, the same reason that the Americans chose Florida for their flight training bases and the French the Mediterranean for theirs.

At the beginning of 1912, Vice Admiral Nikolai O. Essen, commander of the Baltic Fleet at the time, gave orders to Capt. Adrian I. Nepenin, who was head of the *Sluzhba Nabuideniia i Sviazi* (Reconnaissance and Liaison Service), to form an aviation service within that section of the navy. He, in turn, assigned the whole project to Capt. Boris Dudrov – an outstanding graduate of the Russian Naval Academy. Dudrov had been involved in the Russo-Japanese War and had been captured after the fall of Port Arthur. His experiences in battle gave him a new insight into the need for observation and communication.

Boris Dudrov rose to the challenge well. He went to France to familiarise himself with all aspects of flight training and the purchase of the right aircraft. On his return he proceeded to set up bases and organise the right staff to man them. Right from the start Dudrov received strong support and co-operation from Admiral Ivan K. Grigorovich, the Naval Minister, Vice Admirals Aleksander A. Liven and Aleksander I. Rusin.

In 1914, at the outbreak of war, Dudrov was promoted to Chief of the Baltic Fleet's Air Arm and introduced the navy's one and only aviation vessel – *Orlitza*. This Scottish-built ship

An aerial shot of Naval Air Station Sevastapol showing a metal hangar.

was originally a cargo-passenger liner and had been named the *Imperatriza Alexsandra*. It was later renamed *Wologda*, then after conversion to a seaplane-carrier in St Petersburg on 2 February 1915, she was named *Orlitza*. During the First World War *Orlitza* served in the Gulf of Riga and was extremely active in defending against German operations around the Straits of Irben, Osel Island and Moon Sound. *Orlitza* and her aircraft were active throughout the war, then in April 1918 with the uprising in Russia well under way, she was moved from her berth in Helsinki together with other ships of the Baltic Fleet to Kronstadt, Russia.

Little is known of the *Orlitza*'s activities during the Russian Civil War, but it is thought that some of the expertise of her crew was used to organise Bolshevik naval aviation on the Volga. She was put back into mercantile service at the end of 1919 and renamed *Soviet*.

The Russian Naval Air Arm controlled the coastline from St Petersburg to the south-west German section of the frontier. Along the coast a number of seaplane stations sprung up as the war progressed, some with permanent facilities such as concrete ramps and steel hangars, other nothing more that a couple of tents with a wooden mooring dock. The entrance to the Bay of Riga was controlled by two air stations of the islands of Dago and Oesel – they also monitored the south-west coast of Finland and the Åland Islands.

Two other Scottish built cargo-liners, *Imperator Nikolai I* and *Imperator Alexsandr I* were converted into seaplane-carriers, each carrying eight Grigorovich M.9 seaplanes, early in 1915. Originally built for the Russian Steam Navigation Trading Co. for use on the Black Sea – Egyptian trading routes, these sister ships were assigned to the Black Sea Fleet and were involved throughout the First World War.

On 2 May 1915 five aircraft from the *Imperator Nikolai I* carried out a reconnaissance of the coastal batteries of the Bosphorus. The following day aircraft from the *Imperator Nikolai I* and the *Almaz* bombed the town of Igneada causing extensive damage and inflicting a large number of casualties.

The 1st Combat Group consisting of the battleship *Imperatrica Marija*, the cruiser *Kagul*, four destroyers and the seaplane-carriers *Imperator Nikolai I* and *Imperator Alexsandr I*, carried

Russian seaplane carrier Orlitza *with a FBA flying boat in the forward hangar.*

Kite balloon over the forward deck of the Russian armoured cruiser Rossija.

out a combined air and shelling attack on the harbour at Zonguldak, Turkey. A steamer in the harbour was sunk by bombs dropped by seaplanes from the carriers, whilst shells from the ships battered the harbour and the town. Two German submarines, UB-7 and UB-14, were outside the harbour and opened fire on the seaplane-carriers, forcing them to retreat leaving two of their seaplanes behind. What happened to the crews of the seaplanes is not known.

The Turkish Navy was one of the weakest navies of the First World War, so it was the Germans that had to bolster the sparse Turkish fleet with the battle-cruiser *Groben*, renamed *Sultan Yavus Selim*, and the light cruiser *Breslau*, renamed *Midilli*.

Aircraft from the *Imperator Nikolai I* sank the 4,211 ton Turkish collier *Irmingard* off the coast of Varna on 6 February 1916. This was largest merchant ship to be sunk by aircraft during the First World War. Then on 25 August three seaplane-carriers, *Almaz, Imperator Nikolai* and *Imperator Alexsandr,* supported by the battleship *Imperatriza Ekaterina II* and seven destroyers, carried out an attack on German submarines at Varna, Turkey. In retaliation German seaplanes suddenly arrived and carried out bombing raids on the seaplane-carriers and destroyers. The destroyer *Pospesnyj* was badly damaged, but was towed to safety before she could sink. After the war the seaplane-carriers were taken over by the Bolsheviks and renamed. *Imperator Nikolai I* was renamed *Respublikanetz*, whilst *Imperator Alexsandr I* was renamed *Aviator*. Despite all the trouble of renaming both vessels, neither ship moved from its port and during the Allied intervention in the Russian Civil War, both ships were taken over by the French. Once again their names were changed, to *Pierre Loti* and *Lamartine* respectively. They went back to sea with Cie Messageries Maritimes, but during the Second World War both were torpedoed and sunk by German U-boats. Also commandeered by the Bolsheviks was the *Almaz*, who turned her into one of their main headquarters. She was later

Orlitza with the covers down on the forward hangar and furled on her aft hangar.

seized by French forces at Odessa and given to the White Russians. She was taken, along with other ex-Tsarist ships, to Algeria in September 1920 where she stayed until 1928, when she was taken over by the French who then scrapped her in 1934.

After Romania had entered the war, five merchant ships belonging to the Romanian State Maritime Service were requisitioned by the Russians to be converted into aircraft-carrying auxiliaries. They were *Romania, Roate, Regele Carol I, Principesa Maria, Imperator Trayan* and *Dakia*, all of which carried four Grigorovich M.9 seaplanes. The French-built *Romania*, with the other requisitioned merchant ships, joined the Black Sea Fleet in August 1916 and was the only one of the five to be rated *gidrovio* transport (hydroplane transport). She served throughout the remainder of the war in operations off the Bosphorus and Bulgarian coasts. Bombing attacks were carried out on shore installations, ports and reconnaissance missions on troop movements. During the Russian revolution the *Romania* was renamed *Rouminskaya Respublika* and returned to Romania, as were all the other Romanian vessels.

The total number of aircraft possessed by the Russian Navy at the beginning of the First World War, was twenty-four – all seaplanes – a mixture of Curtiss and Grigorovich. This included a float version of the four-engined Sikorsky Ilya Mourmetz. By the end of the war the Black Sea Fleet had under its control over 200 aircraft, the majority of which were Grigorovich M.5, M.9, M.11 and M.15 seaplanes. The rest of the aircraft fleet consisted of a few Nieuport fighters.

Although the Russians went to surprising lengths to develop the use of aircraft on ships, including the converting of a petroleum barge that could carry nine Grigorovich M.9 seaplanes and had a flight deck that covered over ninety per cent of the 460ft deck, they never quite mastered it. During the Second World War, both Russia and Germany made attempts to develop aircraft carriers, none of which came to fruition.

Russian Naval Aircraft of the First World War

Curtiss Flying Boats	Grigorovich M.5
Engels Flying Boat	Grigorovich M.9
FBA (Franco British Aviation) Type H	Grigorovich M.11
fighters	Grigorovich M.15
	Grigorovich M.16

The Russian seaplane-carrier Imperator Nikolai I.

The Russian seaplane carrier Almaz *that carried four aircraft on her deck.*

Battleship Imperator Alexsandr III.

An FBA flying boat being hoisted aboard the seaplane carrier Orlitza.

An FBA flying boat of the Black Sea fleet displaying the naval cross of St Andrew on the rudder.

A Maurice Farman Shorthorn (MFII) as used by the Baltic and Black Sea fleets.

An FBA flying boat of the Black Sea fleet.

A Maurice Farman floatplane No.M-14 of the Baltic Sea fleet.

The carpenter's shop inside one of the large hangars at the Revel Naval Air Station on the Baltic Sea.

Curtiss Triads on the concrete dock at Naval Air Station Sevastapol.

A Curtiss Triad of the Black Sea fleet at Sevastapol.

A Henri Farman HF.22 seaplane of the Black Sea fleet.

Grigorovich M.9 floatplane about to be hoisted aboard the Imperator Nikolai I.

A Nieuport 9 fighter belonging to the Baltic Sea fleet.

A Maurice Farman Shorthorn floatplane at Revel Naval Air Station.

Kolyma *releases her observation balloon at Vladivostok in 1904.*

Rossija *at Vladivostok with the kite balloon she used for reconnaissance sorties.*

The converted liner Imperator Alexandr I *with Grigorovich M.9 flying boats on her stern section.*

A Grigorovich M.9 seaplane being hoisted aboard the Almaz.

Three of the Russian Black Sea Fleet's seaplane carriers, from left to right: Romania, Imperator Nikolai I *and* Imperator Alexandr I.

9
Italian Naval Air Service

The Italians, although not famed for their aviation exploits, were responsible for some of the earliest excursions into aerial warfare, including being one of the first countries in the world to convert a ship to an aviation-vessel. In 1907 the Italians equipped their cruiser with a kite balloon to enable them to carry out manoeuvres off Sicily. After a number of successful flights the project was shelved, but resurrected in 1911 during the Italy/Turkish conflict.

The brigantine *Cavalmarino* was requisitioned, stripped of her second mast and rigging and converted to carry a kite balloon. Unable to sail under her own power, the *Cavalmarino* was towed by the naval tug *Ercole*. During the conflict the kite balloon was used to spot gunfire for the battleship *Re Umberto* as she pounded the Turkish shore positions off the North African coast. After a degree of success the use of the kite balloon was ended abruptly when, during a horrendous storm, it was swept off the deck of the battleship. Such was the ferocity of the storm that the kite balloon was not found for two days and, when finally discovered on a beach, was found to be virtually shredded and beyond repair.

Plans were also drawn up by Capitano de Genio Navale Allesandro Guidoni to convert an old cruiser, the *Piemonte*, into a seaplane carrier. Together with Marquis Raul Pateras Pescara a number of attempts were made to develop a torpedo aircraft.

In 1913 the Italian naval air arm, Sezione Aviazione Marina, was formed and equipped entirely with foreign aircraft. No thought appears to have been given to carrying these aircraft on board warships, but experiments were carried out carrying a seaplane on the battleship *Dante Alighieri* and the cruiser *San Marco*. None of these experiments amounted to anything – then in May 1915, Italy was drawn into the First World War.

Italian A-Class airship in foreground.

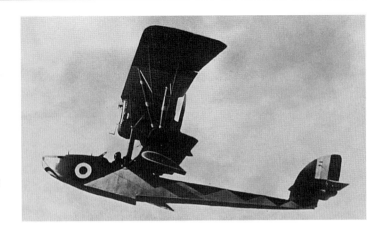

*Macchi M.5 single-seat
flying boat of the
Italian Navy.*

Italy's naval air arm at this time consisted of thirty aircraft, which included three seaplanes attached to the cruiser *Elba*. All of Italy's aircraft were of foreign design and manufacture, but then appeared the Macchi L.I built by the newly developed aircraft division of the coach-building company Societé Anonima Nieuport-Macchi at Varese. The Macchi L.I was almost an exact copy of an Austro-Hungarian Lohner flying boat that had been captured earlier.

The Lohner was a good flying boat and the designers at Nieuport-Macchi were quick to exploit all the good points and improve all the bad points of the aircraft. It wasn't long before they were producing their own Macchi flying boats and a number of other types. In fact, within one year the majority of aircraft used by the naval air arm were Italian.

The narrow confines of the Adriatic restricted the size of any seaplane-carriers and Italy only had two ships capable of carrying aircraft, the *Elba* and the *Europa*. There were two other kite balloon-carrying vessels, the lighters *Umberto Missana* and *Luigi Mina*, both just over 200 tons, but they were restricted to coastal patrols in the Adriatic. The *Europa* was the former British merchant ship *Manila* and had a variety of names and owners before being purchased by the Italian Navy for conversion to a submarine depot ship. It was then decided to utilise the derricks onboard the ship for recovering seaplanes and so the ship was converted to a seaplane-carrier. Converted at La Spezia Royal Navy Yard, the *Europa* was commissioned on 6 October 1915 and stationed at Brindisi until the beginning of 1916. Then she was moved to the Albanian port of Valona where she remained as a harbour-based tender until the end of the war. Her complement of aircraft consisted of six fighter aircraft and two reconnaissance craft.

The role played by the naval air arm of the Italian Navy was not exactly awe-inspiring, but they caused the rest of the world to sit up and take notice of what a small country can do when faced with more powerful adversaries. With the establishment of the Regia Aeronautica, the naval air arm disappeared and was absorbed into one air force.

Italian aircraft and Airships of the First World War

A-Class airship
Airship M-1 of the Italian Navy
FBA (Franco British Aviation) Type H fighter
Macchi M.5 single-seat fighter

Italian airship M-1 of the Italian Navy.

The Europa *showing the side of her hangars partially open.*

The converted brigantine Cavalmarino *with its kite balloon.*

The Italian seaplane carrier Europa. *The suspended aircraft types are FBA Type Hs and a Macchi M.5 fighter.*

Crew of an Italian FBA being rescued by the crew of a ship seen here aboard the ship's boat, with their aircraft under tow, and being rowed back to the main ship.

10
The Japanese Naval Air Service

Although the Imperial Japanese Navy had used a balloon as an observation platform for the purposes of artillery spotting for the shore-based battery at Port Arthur during the Russo-Japanese War in 1904, it lacked any formal air organisation. Bitter inter-service rivalry between the Imperial Japanese Army and the Imperial Japanese Navy caused the latter to form its own aviation service, *Kaigun Kokujutsu Kenkyu Kai* (Naval Committee for Aeronautical Research), early in 1912. The committee promptly dispatched three lieutenants to France and three to America for flight training. Those sent to America were authorised to purchase two suitable aircraft. The aircraft selected were a Curtiss seaplane and Farman float-plane which were shipped to Yokosuka, Japan, and used to train pilots. Lt Yozo Kaneko came back with two Maurice Farman aircraft, whilst Lt Sankichi Kohno returned from America with two Curtiss seaplanes. On 2 November 1912 the first flights of these new aircraft were made from the naval base at Yokosuka. The year also saw the first 'aircraft carrier'. The Japanese merchant ship *Wakamiya Maru* was crudely fitted out to carry seaplanes and had the distinction of being the first aircraft carrier to participate in a war.

When the First World War broke out in Europe, the Japanese Naval Air Force consisted of four Maurice Farman seaplanes and seven pilots. The simple construction of the Farmans were soon copied by the Yokosuka Naval Arsenal and designated Navy Type Mo Small Seaplane. Then, on 23 August 1914, Japan declared war on Germany and the Imperial

The Japanese seaplane carrier Wakamiya Maru *seen here with a Maurice Farman floatplane taxiing toward the ship to be picked up.*

Japanese Naval and Army aircraft went on a combined offensive against the German enclave at Tsing-tao on the Chinese mainland during September and October 1914. Admiral Kato Sadakichi's fleet lay siege to the German protectorate. Reconnaissance flights were made and the German battleship *Kaiserin Elisabeth* attacked, but only a mine-laying ship was sunk. A number of artillery shells were fitted with crudely made metal fins or cloth streamers in an effort to stabilise the shell as it was dropped from the aircraft. A few lucky ones managed to explode close to their intended target, but the vast majority made no impact. As time went on, however, improvements were made in bomb sights and racks which improved the accuracy of these crude devices.

The first reconnaissance flight was made on 5 September 1914 when Lt Hideho Wada in Maurice Farman and Sub-Lt Madsaru Fujise, in a two-seat Maurice Farman, flew over Chiao-chou Bay in search of the German cruiser *Emden*. They did not find the cruiser, but among other information gleaned, they spotted a number of other vessels at anchor in the bay. The information received showed the advantages of having reconnaissance aircraft as this information was acquired in a matter of hours, not in the number of days that it usually took.

On 13 October 1914 the first aerial contact took place, when a German Rumpler Taube was spotted by three Army Farmans whilst on a reconnaissance flight. The three Japanese aircraft dived to attack the Rumpler Taube, which was flown by Sub-Lt Günther Pluschow, but were unable catch it. The Rumpler Taube later landed at Haichow in China to refuel, but the neutral Chinese made moves to seize the aircraft so Pluschow set fire to it to prevent it falling into enemy hands.

A handful of Japanese Army pilots were sent to France during the war but it is thought that they did not see combat. A Japanese-born RFC pilot – Flt Sgt O'Hara – flew on the Western Front and was wounded six times. It is not recorded if he shot down any enemy aircraft.

After the war the Imperial Japanese Navy, which had studied the development of the Royal Naval Air Service with great interest, hired British aeronautical engineers from the Sopwith Aviation Co. They designed the first Japanese carrier aircraft for the first purpose-built aircraft carrier *Hosho Swooping Dragon* which was commissioned in 1922. Laid down as an oil tanker, work was stopped just six months after work had begun and the project switched to the building of an aircraft carrier aided by the British Technical Mission.

The Japanese Navy's contribution to the First World War was minimal, although they did fly forty-nine missions, and it did give the West an insight into the structure and development of the Japanese military machine.

Japanese Aircraft of the First World War

Curtiss Flying Boats
Maurice Farmans
Yokosho Navy Type Mo small seaplane (Copy of the Maurice Farman seaplane)
Yokosho Navy Type Mo large seaplane (Copy of the Maurice Farman seaplane)
Yokosho Navy Type Ka seaplane (Copy of the Curtiss 1912 version seaplane)
Yokosho Experimental Japanese Navy Type seaplane
Yokosho Experimental Nakajima Tractor seaplane

A Yokosho Navy Type Mo large seaplane, based on the Maurice Farman seaplane.

The first Japanese Navy seaplane, the Yokosho Experimental Japanese Navy Type seaplane.

The Wakamiya Maru *with both her fore and aft canvas hangars furled.*

A Yokosho Navy Type Mo small seaplane. This a copy of the Maurice Farman seaplane.

A Yokosho Navy Type Ka seaplane, based on the Curtiss 1912 version seaplane.

The experimental Yokosho Nakajima Tractor seaplane.

11
German Naval Air Service

The aviation arm of Imperial Germany was not a separate branch of the armed forces but a section of the Army – the officers and enlisted men who joined were, therefore, merely a detachment. The naval arm of the Imperial German Air Service was split into two organisations: Marine Luftschiffe-Abteilung which covered the whole naval airship service; and Marine-Fliegerabteilung which covered everything pertaining to aircraft and establishments. The vast majority of the naval aircraft were grouped under Marine Lanflieger and assigned to various home defence commands and seaplane bases.

German seaplane bases existed before the war at Putzig, Kiel, Wilhelmshaven and Heligoland. Of the four bases only Kiel and Putzig were maintained at full strength because the total complement of officers and men in the air arm at that time was less than 200. At the onset of the war a fully manned unit, complete with two Friedrichshafens, four officers (three pilots and one deck officer) and fifty-five other ranks, was dispatched to set up a station at Zeebrugge.

Aviation at the time was deemed to be so insignificant that those who chose to be detached to the aviation units wore their ordinary unit uniforms. Rittmeister Manfred Freiherr von Richthofen for instance wore his Uhlan uniform, Leutnant Oswald Boelke the grey uniform of the infantry, and Kapitänleutnant Friedrich Christiansen the dark blue of the Imperial German Navy. The one thing that distinguished them from all the other military personnel was that those attached to the aviation section had a small propeller affixed to the shoulder boards on their uniforms, and after qualifying wore their pilot/observer badge on the lower left side of their respective jackets.

The hangar containing the LZ.38 at Evère burning fiercely after being bombed by aircraft of the RNAS.

Count von Zeppelin on board the LZ.30 on 28 May 1916. The officer with Zeppelin is Hauptmann Macher.

Even then there were differences in the badges that each service awarded its pilots and observers. The Army aviation badge, for instance, had an aeroplane in flight depicted in its centre, surrounded by an oval oak wreath in silver with the Imperial crown on top. The observers badge was similar in design and shape, but in the centre was a black and red checkerboard. The Naval pilot's badge was also of an oval shape with an oak wreath with the Imperial crown on top but made in a gold-coloured metal. In the centre of the badge was depicted a sea eagle in flight over Heligoland and the surrounding sea, whilst the Naval observer's badge was largely the same, but with a sea eagle sitting on a craggy cliff overlooking the sea. The Zeppelin badge, although the same in design as the Naval one, depicted an airship in its centre.

Unlike the Army, the observers in the naval aviation service were all enlisted men, whilst the pilots were mainly officers. In the formative years of German Army Air Service, all pilots had been enlisted men whilst the observers were officers – a throwback to the days when the upper classes were chauffeured around. Early into the war this attitude changed very quickly when the Army pilots saw themselves as Teutonic Knights riding to war. It was an accepted fact, however, that those joining the aviation service risked losing out on promotion from their respective regiments – out of sight, out of mind!

One of the other idiosyncrasies of the German Navy at the time was that naval officers who belonged to the unrestricted line of officer corps, that is to say that they were seamen, had the words '*zur See*' after their rank – unlike the other naval officers who belonged to the naval artillery, medical, engineering and infantry sections. The seamen group was also the

Lt Cdr Mathy of the Zeppelin L.31.

Kapitänleutnant Pieter Strasser of the Zeppelin L.70.

The burnt-out hangar of the LZ.38 after the bombing attack by RNAS aircraft.

only one allowed to wear the naval officer's dirk, initiated by the Tsar of Russia. All other groups had to wear the long sabre, although this was later replaced by a short bayonet with a sword knot attached. For obvious reasons the wearing of a long sabre when entering the cockpit of an aeroplane had its own problems. When Kapitänleutnant Friedrich Christiansen was awarded the Orden Pour le Mérite on 11 December 1917 it was hoped he would go into the *zur See* officers' group – Christiansen declined the offer and wore his uniform with the long sabre of naval artillery.

German naval aviation began on 10 March 1910, when Naval Engineer Karl Loew was awarded his German Flying Certificate. He was quickly followed by a further four Naval Engineers who all qualified as pilots. During the formative years a number of seaplanes were acquired from other countries, among them the British Avro, Sopwith and Curtiss models. It is interesting to note that during the First World War, the German press printed a photograph of a 'captured' Sopwith Batboat which in fact had been purchased some years before the war had actually started.

In October 1910 Großadmiral Alfred von Tirpitz ordered the investigation of heavier-than-air machines for naval use. He allocated 200,000 marks for research by the Kaierliche

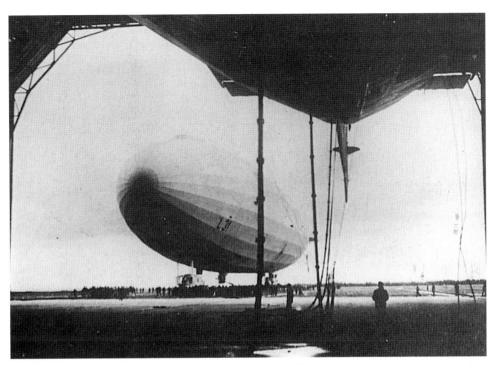

The Zeppelin L.31 being 'walked' out of its hangar at Nordholz.

The L.33 overflying the German battleship SMS Heligoland *at the Battle of Jutland.*

Werft at Danzig into the design and development of seaplanes. They produced an Albatros pusher aircraft with a single float. Other manufacturers were approached to design and aircraft for the navy, but they were most reluctant when they found out that the navy insisted on all their aircraft being amphibians.

The navy suddenly got unexpected support from Großadmiral Prinz Heinrich of Prussia, younger brother of the Kaiser, who had had an interest in aviation for many years and recently gained his pilot's licence. Prinz Heinrich supported Tirpitz enthusiastically, putting his considerable influence behind him.

With the outbreak of war came the creation of flying sections, the Naval Flying Section at Kiel-Holtenhau under the command of Commander Cygas and the Volunteer Naval Flying Corps at Berlin-Johnisthal under the command of Leutnant Commander Golz. A further three stations were formed at Heligoland, Warnemünde and Putzig. The station at Warnemünde became the SVK (Seeflugzeug-Versuchs-Kommando) where German seaplanes were tested and captured Allied seaplanes evaluated. It also carried tests on the use of torpedo-carrying aircraft together with TVA (Torpedo-Versuchs-Ansalt) at Kiel Friedrichsort.

The role of German naval aviation was placed under the control of the Naval High Command and one officer appointed to be in charge – Admiral von Schröder. He in turn separated the landplanes, seaplanes and airships and appointed group commanding officers or the three sections, one of these was Kapitänleutnant von Tschirski und von Bögendorf. It was the airship section that the Navy concentrated on, although they did have some successes with their fighter/bomber section.

Against the wishes of his naval advisers, Kaiser Wilhelm appointed his brother Großadmiral Prinz Heinrich to Commander of Naval Forces in the Baltic (*Oberbefehlshaber der Ostseestreitkräfte*). To everyone's surprise Prinz Heinrich turned out to be more that just competent leader, but one fully conversant with what was required in such a situation. He made extensive use of aircraft and airships, including putting aircraft on the armoured cruiser Friedrich Carl for reconnaissance purposes over the Russian coast. This was the first example of aircraft accompanying a task force.

Experiments were also carried out using an aircraft for mine-laying operations, the first time an aircraft had ever been used.

The man responsible for the birth of the German airship was Count Ferdinand von Zeppelin. He had joined the Army in 1857 and was commissioned a Leutnant. In 1863 he was sent as an official observer with the Union Army during the American Civil War. During his time with the Union Army he was impressed with the role of the tethered balloon for observation purposes. He returned to Germany to fight in the Austro-German War and the Franco-Prussian War for which he was both decorated and admonished. During the Franco-Prussian War, it is said that von Zeppelin deserted the patrol that he was leading when it came under heavy fire. All his men were killed during the engagement, and had he not returned with vital information, there is no doubt that he would have been court-martialled. He left the Army in 1891 with the rank of Leutnantgeneral, but under a cloud. The precise reason has never been disclosed but it is believed the he openly criticised some of the Kaiser's closest friends on a number of sensitive military and political matters.

Von Zeppelin, although apparently never openly showing an interest in aviation, then concentrated his efforts on developing a free-moving rigid airship. His first airship, the LZ.1, was built in 1900 and first flew, if that can be the term, on 2 July of that year. The LZ.1 had an overall length of 420ft, a diameter of 38ft 6in, contained 400,000cu.ft of hydrogen and was

The crew of the Zeppelin LZ.38 – the first crew to bomb London.

powered by two 16hp Daimler marine engines. The airship was towed out of its hangar on Lake Constance and cast off. It rose to a height of over 1,000ft and for $1\frac{1}{4}$ hours the airship remained airborne. There was some response to the helm, but that was severely restricted because of the two minute rudders at the stern and at the bow. Vertical control of the airship was maintained using a sliding weight mechanism. This was achieved by moving a 550lb weight fore and aft between the two passenger cars suspended beneath the airship. Problems arose with the sliding weight and the airship was returned to its floating hangar. His next airship the LZ.2, which although handling extremely well, suffered an engine problem that resulted in the airship drifting away and crashing near the town of Kisslegg where it was destroyed. A new airship was built – the LZ.3. This time the German government took an interest and awarded Count von Zeppelin 500,000 marks (£25,000 at the time). Up to this point all research and development had been financed by von Zeppelin and his friends, but now with government backing the pace was stepped up. The government ordered two Zeppelin airships, the LZ.3 being one of them and the LZ.4.

Confidence was growing in von Zeppelin's venture so much so that the King and Queen of Württemberg were taken on a flight, the first time any member of a royal family had flown, in essence giving it the stamp of royal approval.

On 4 August 1908, the LZ.4 took off on a twenty-four-hour test flight. On board was Count von Zeppelin and ten others. The flight went well until one of the engines failed. After emergency repairs the flight continued, but broke down again. This time von Zeppelin managed to get the airship to Daimler's plant for them to make the repairs to the engine. Unfortunately as they approached the ground, soldiers took hold of the mooring lines and because of their inexperience in handling such a craft, mishandled the airship causing it to crash into the ground and catch fire. The mangled mess of wreckage would have spelled disaster for most men, but it seemed to inspire the now seventy-year-old von Zeppelin. The government, realising that there was a future in airships, aided von Zeppelin financially, helping him create DELAG (the Deutsche Luftschiffahrts-Aktien-Gesellschaft).

The only airship that von Zeppelin had left was the LZ.3, which was in the process of being refurbished. The army wanted to have their own airship and took over the LZ.3 before the tests were completed. All Zeppelins have always been known by their original numbering of LZ by the army and just 'L' by the navy.

Von Zeppelin produced the next airship for the army, LZ.5. Again bad luck dogged von Zeppelin and during tests it too crashed. Quickly repaired, it was handed over to the army for tests but, after a bad landing during increasing high winds that ripped her apart, she was totally destroyed.

The next airship, LZ.6 was undoubtedly one of the best. It ironed out most of the problems that beset the earlier airships and during one cross-country trip, on 25 August 1909, carried Count von Zeppelin, a number of government officials and one distinguished passenger – Orville Wright. It would have been interesting to eavesdrop on the conversation between the two major exponents of the heavier-than-air and the lighter-than air craft of that time, but unfortunately no record exists of the conversation between them.

The first German Navy Zeppelin, L.1 (formerly the LZ.14), was completed in 1912 but crashed less than six months later in the North Sea on 9 September 1913 killing the head of the Naval Airship Division, Korvettenkapitän Friedrich Metzing. The second naval Zeppelin, L.2, did not fare much better. It was lost when it caught fire during altitude tests on its tenth flight. There were no survivors. These disasters undermined Großadmiral von Tirpitz's faith in the airship and he appointed Korvettenkapitän Peter Strasser to take over as head of the Naval Airship Division. Strasser set about trying to build the Airship Division back up and persuaded von Tirpitz that the division needed another airship. With great reluctance von Tirpitz ordered a third Zeppelin, the L.3, so that the Airship Division could at least have one airship on which to train.

Zeppelin was not alone in airship manufacturing in Germany. Another company, founded in 1909 by Dr Ing E.H. Johann Schütte, the Luftschiffbau Schütte-Lanz was offering strong competition. Dr Schütte, a trained naval architect and engineer, was backed by two of Germany's top industrialists, Dr Karl Lanz and August Röchling. Schütte's designs were far

Hansa-Brandenburg W-29s of C-Staffel flying from their base at Zeebrugge. This Staffel was commanded by Friedrich Christiansen.

The L.2 airship on fire whilst coming in to land. Seconds later the airship exploded. The ground crew can be seen running for their lives.

The Zeppelin hangar at Tondern ablaze after being bombed by RNAS aircraft.

A Rumpler 6B-1 fighter seaplane demonstrating its manoeuvrability.

in advance of von Zeppelin's, but they suffered greatly because of his choice of materials. He favoured a type of plywood held together with casein glue for the girders that made up the framework. This was chosen for the greatest possible lightness, but the wood was found to suffer badly from dampness and humidity, causing the framework to soften and come loose and ultimately fall apart.

The company manufactured twenty airships in all: eleven for the army and nine for the navy. But their vulnerability became apparent when the army lost nearly all their airships during the early part of First World War, from either ground fire or structural disintegration. The navy fared little better and turned to von Zeppelin for their airships.

The Navy, at the start of the war, was the proud possessor of one airship – the L.3. There was no shortage of volunteers – Hugo Eckner, for example, who had been with Count von Zeppelin almost from the beginning, volunteered for flying duties with the Navy but was refused. Eckner had been in the Army and had reached the rank of sergeant before being honourably discharged. But not coming from an upper-class family placed a barrier between him and the officer class, which prevented him acquiring a commission, despite his having a greater knowledge of airships that most of the naval personnel in the airship division. The Navy recognised this and offered him an honorary rank of Korvettenkapitän (lieutenant-commander) and put him in charge of training for airship personnel – but he was not allowed to wear the uniform befitting his rank. Although stung by this snobbery Hugo Eckner nevertheless threw himself into his new role delighted to discover that his old friend Pieter Strasser was to work with him. In fact in September 1913 Strasser was called to Naval Headquarters, Berlin, and was given command, much to his surprise, of naval Zeppelins. The original commander, Korvettenkapitän Matzing, had been lost some months earlier with his crew, when the L.1 had crashed in the North Sea whilst on a training flight.

Naval aviation, even during its infancy, was not adverse to looking at different ways to exploit the use of the aeroplane. A little over eighty years ago, a handful of officers in the Imperial German Navy began to look into the possibilities of operating aircraft from submarines, although at that time there was no operational requirement to do so. Rather it

Hansa-Brandenburg W-12 (top) together with a Friedrichshafen FF-49c on patrol.

Albatros W-1 seaplane, also known as the Albatros WDD, of 1914.

was a case of personal initiative, circumstance and the availability of a Friedrichshafen FF.29 twin-float, single-engined seaplane.

During the early stages of the First World War, the German Army quickly overran Belgium and the port of Zeebrugge was soon in German hands, becoming a base well suited to operations by U-boats. The base commander, and U-boat captain, Oberleutnant zur See Friedrich von Arnauld de la Perierem, who unusually happened to be an aviator also, together with Oberleutnant zur See Walter Forstman, commander of the U-12, both later to become 'Ace' U-boat commanders, were seized with the offensive spirit, and were determined to find out whether the radius of action of a seaplane could be usefully extended by using the submarine as a seaplane transporter. The nearest point on the enemy coast, North Foreland in Kent, lay some seventy-three miles away.

Despite it being midwinter, on 6 January 1915, the seaplane, with its 57ft wingspan, was lashed down athwartships to the foredeck of the U-12 and the unlikely pair sailed out into the harbour to carry out trials. The bows were trimmed down, the aircraft was subsequently floated off and taxied away – all within the protection afforded by the long breakwater of the Zeebrugge Mole. It was decided to continue with the trials immediately.

The strange and vulnerable combination, with the aircraft lashed athwartships and the U-12's two heavy Korting oil engines leaving a tell-tale plume of smoke, headed for the open sea.

A Rumpler 6B-1 seaplane.

Despite a heavy swell, the situation was about manageable. Some thirty miles offshore, the U-boat's commander flooded the forward tanks and released the aircraft which was able to take off successfully. With von Arnauld de la Periere and his observer, Herman Mall, aboard, they flew along the coast of Kent undetected before returning to Zeebrugge directly, rather than making the agreed rendezvous with the U-12 in weather which had deteriorated further. At the debrief, Forstman and von Arnauld considered the whole exercise a complete success but agreed that after the difficulties in getting the aircraft launched, the seas needed to be calmer and the aircraft more secure on the deck.

This remarkable trial conducted in wartime, virtually in the enemy's backyard, was designed to establish a strike capability with small bombs, if not at the heartland then at least at the coastal towns of the enemy. Soon the Friedrichshafen FF.29 had been adapted to carry 12kg bombs and, during the year, twenty-six raids were flown against British and French targets. On Christmas Day 1915, a Friedrichshafen FF.29 flew along the River Thames to Erith on the outskirts of London and dropped two bombs. It was fortunate that they fell without causing injury and damage. Three British aircraft chased the FF 29 without success and it returned safely. The German airmen or 'Zeebrugge Flers' as they were called, had more problems from their own aircraft than they did from the British. On many occasions their seaplanes were forced to land with fouled ignitions or fuel line stoppages. Because of the limited range of their aircraft, many of the more important targets were beyond reach. Understandably, the frustrations of the aircraft crews created morale problems; the problems were recognised by the U-boat officers, however, because they also shared the dangers of operating relatively new and untried weapons, and duly a common bond sprang up between them.

Combined trials of aircraft and submarine had continued sporadically, but high level support was not forthcoming. No doubt this was a correct decision given the vulnerability of the combination and the unreliability endemic in these early aeroplanes. A report to the German High Command on the future of submarine launched aircraft, was thoroughly investigated, and the decision was made that the project be dropped. Von Arnauld was told, 'U-boats operate in the sea, aircraft in the air – there is no connection between the two'.

This minor setback, however, did not prevent the German Navy from exploring aviation. The main thrust of the Naval aviation section was to carry out reconnaissance duties and for this purpose the airship was introduced for the role. Later the airship was to carry out bombing missions against the Allies – sometimes successfully, sometimes disastrously.

The Zeppelins, as the German airships were colloquially known, started their part in the war on reconnaissance flights over the North Sea, but it was quickly realised that they had a greater potential for carrying out bombing raids on England. The first raids however were carried out by aircraft from the Army section just before Christmas 1914. Then on the night of 19/20 January 1915, two naval airships – the L.3, commanded by Kapitänleutnant Hans Fritze, and L.4, commanded by Kapitänleutnant Graf von Platen Hallermund – left the ground at Fuhlsbüttel with orders to join up with L.6, commanded by Oberleutnant zur See Horst Freiherr Treusch von Buttlar-Brandenfels who had lifted off from Nordholz. The L.3 and L.4 crossed the English coast and dropped nine incendiary bombs from a height of 3,000ft on the town of Yarmouth, killing two of its inhabitants and wounding several more. One of the bombs fell just fifty yards from a hall packed with Army reservists, fortunately causing no injury or damage. The L.6 developed engine trouble when a crankshaft failed five hours into the flight and had to return to Nordholz. Both the other airships returned safely, however the L.3 later crashed during a reconnaissance flight.

A rare combat photograph of the 1914-1918 war showing a Hansa-Brandenburg W-29 of C-Staffel attacking a British Felixstowe F-2A flying boat on the water.

A Hansa-Brandenburg W-29 flying boat flying over its base at Norderney.

On 26 February 1915 Kapitänleutnant Helmut Beelitz, commander of the L.8, took off from Düsseldorf on an attempted a raid on Britain but aborted because of engine trouble. He tried again on 4 March, this time from Gontrode, Belgium, and again he was troubled with engine problems. The next attempt was by the L.9 commanded by Kapitänleutnant Heinrich Mathy. The flight started out initially as a reconnaissance mission, although the airship was carrying bombs, but as the weather was so favourable Mathy decided to ask permission to carry out a raid on Britain. After receiving authorisation he headed the Zeppelin across the English Channel toward Newcastle. The raid, although not successful in terms of damage and casualties, was a morale boost for the Germans after Mathy had claimed to have hit shipyards and industrial areas – neither of which was true. This prompted Fregattenkäpitan Peter Strasser, who was head of the Naval Airship Division, to set up another raid the following day. Three Zeppelins were prepared for the flight, L.5, L.6 and L.7. The L.5, which led the attack, was commanded by Kapitänleutnant der Reserve Aloys Böcker, Oberleutnant von Buttlar Brandenfels commanded the L.6 and Oberleutnant zur See Werner Peterson in the L.7. The L.5 opened the attack by dropping bombs on Southwold, Suffolk and Henham Hall, causing minimal damage. Böcker then dropped bombs on Lowestoft – the only damage being to a timber yard. The L.6 headed for Maldon and Heybridge, Essex, and bombed two houses from a height of 5,000ft – where again the damage was only minimal. The height was also low enough for the Zeppelin to be attacked by gunfire and rifle fire from the ground, and indeed, when von Buttlar and his crew returned, they discovered that two of the L.6 cells had received numerous hits and were leaking badly. The L.7 on the other hand, with Peter Strasser on board, reached England but because of strong headwinds had only managed to skirt along the coast and so had turned back without dropping their bombs.

At the end of May 1915 the Army Zeppelin LZ.38 carried out the first raid on London killing seven people, injuring thirty-five others and causing extensive damage. The fact that British aircraft had been sent up to intercept and anti-aircraft guns had not fired one shot, caused great elation amongst the Zeppelin crews, but a great deal of bitterness and anger was felt by the Londoners. The German Navy felt that they should have been the first to carry out such a raid and commenced to plan one for 4 June. The L.10, commanded by Kapitänleutnant Klaus Hirsch, and SL.3 (*Schütte Lanz*), commanded by Kapitänleutnant Fritz Boemack, lifted off and headed across the English Channel. Hirsch, on reaching the Thames Estuary and believing he was over Harwich, unloaded his bombs – but it was actually Gravesend. The bombs destroyed the Yacht Club, which was being used as a military hospital, inflicting some injuries but no fatalities. The German commander later laid claim to having 'caused a large number of fires to break out all over Harwich including either a gas works or oil tank, judging by the explosion' – none of which was true.

The SL.3 managed to get as far as Flamborough Head, with the intention of carrying out a bombing raid on Hull. Fortunately for the residents of Hull, the airship encountered very strong headwinds and was unable to make any progress. Boemack, conscious of the fact that he was in a very vulnerable position, decided that it would be more prudent to retreat. He dropped three bombs as a form of defiant gesture and headed back across the North Sea for Nordholz. The three bombs that were dropped exploded harmlessly in a field.

At the end of 1914 Germany had requisitioned two cargo-passenger ships, *Ansawald* and *Santa Elena*, for conversion by the Danzig Kaiserliche Werft to seaplane-carriers. Even after extensive modifications they were deemed to be unstable, and so had to undergo even more modifications before being accepted on 17 July 1915. Designated *Flugzeugmutterschiffe* ('aeroplane mother ship') I and II respectively, neither of the ships were considered to be fast and so were basically seaplane depot ships rather that seaplane-carriers. In October 1917 the *Santa Elena* (FS.II) had her first taste of action, when her Friedrichshafen FF.33s flew bombing missions against Russian emplacements and vessels along the Courland coast. Later her aircraft were involved in the seizure of Oesel, Moon Island and Dago Island during Operation Albion.

The *Answald* (FS.I) was based mainly at Libau in the Baltic and her aircraft used mainly for reconnaissance purposes. Like *Santa Elena* her aircraft were Friedrichshafen 29 and 33s.

The German seaplane carrier SMS Answald *with one of her aircraft being prepared for launching, the other already in the sea about to take off.*

A Hansa-Brandenburg W-29 fighter seaplane.

The German commerce raider Wolf *with her aircraft* Wölfchen *on the deck.*

The German seaplane carrier SMS Santa Elena *with two of her aircraft in their furled hangars.*

A Friedrichshafen FF.33E being lowered from its hangar aboard the SMS Santa Elena.

Hansa-Brandenburg W.12 of Christiansen's Staffel on patrol.

At the end of the war she surrendered to Britain, was renamed *Vulcan City* and reverted back to being a cargo-passenger vessel. She was scrapped in 1933.

There was a third *Flugzeugmutterschiffe* – FS.III. This was British ship *Oswestry* which found herself interned at Danzig at the beginning of the war. She was ignored until 1917 when she was renamed *Oswald* and used as a minesweeper. In July 1918 she was converted to a seaplane-carrier and designated FS.III and stationed in Ore Sound at the southern end of the Kattegat between Denmark and Sweden. Capable of carrying four Friedrichshafen FF.33 aircraft, she provided escort to submarines returning from patrol. After the war she was sold to the Japanese, renamed *Eian Maru*, and was sunk by American aircraft in July 1945.

Another British ship, the Glasgow-built *Glyndwr*, was also interned in Danzig at the beginning of the war. She was seized by the Germans in December 1914, who incidentally retained her name, and turned her into a seaplane pilot training vessel complete with two Friedrichshafen 29 aircraft. No hangars were installed in the ship and all aircraft operated from the deck. Her complement of aircraft was increased from two to four in January 1915 and operated in the Baltic together with the seaplane-carrier *Santa Elena*. Damaged by a mine in June 1915, the *Glyndwr* underwent extensive repair as was laid up for six months. On returning to active service she operated in the Ore Sound but the damage caused by the mine was causing problems. She was relegated to being used as a mine depot and searchlight barrier vessel. At the end of the war she was given a complete overhaul by the British and sold to a Greek shipping line, which she remained with until she was scrapped in the late 1950s.

Along the coast from Scheveningen, Holland, and down as far as Zeebrugge, Belgium, the naval landplanes and seaplanes were stationed. The seaplane stations that covered the Baltic area, came under the command of I Seeflieger-Abteilung at Appenrade, Kiel, Warnemünde, Rügen, Putzig/Danzig, Liebau, Oesel and Riga. Stations under the command of II Seeflieger-Abteilung were List auf Sylt, Heligoland, Wilhelmshaven, Norderney and Borkum. Other naval seaplane units that covered the Flanders front were at I Seeflugstation at Zeebrugge,

An aerial shot of the SMS Santa Elena.

The first prototype of the Friedrichshafen FF31 seen here without armament.

under the command of Kapitänleutnant Friedrich Christiansen, and II Seeflugstation at Ostend. These were placed under one single command together with the landplane unit at Nieu-Munster and the fighters bases at Westkerke.

The Air Arm of the German Navy in Flanders was made in the following units:

Marine Feldfl.Abtl	Artillery observation and reconnaissance units for the shore-based naval forces.
Küstenstaffeln	Stationed on the coast to direct the fire of the heavy shore batteries.
Schutzstaffeln	Squadrons who carried out escort duties for the aircraft who directed the fire for the heavy shore batteries.
Jagdgeschwader	This unit consisted of five Jagdstaffeln for fighting over the Front.
Seefrostaffel	A unit specifically formed for fighting over the sea.
Fliegermeldung	An Intelligence flying unit.
Stabsbildabteilung	Photographic unit.

One of the commanding officers of the naval air station at Putzig was Kapitänleutnant Alfred Edler. He was an experienced pilot with an expertise in field of torpedo planes. The part of the war was with I Seeflieger-Abteilung in 1914, followed one year later with II Seeflieger-Abteilung. In 1917 he became the commanding officer at Putzig which also housed the I Torpedo-Flieger-Staffel where he used his experience with the use of torpedo aircraft by carrying out a number of trials. His experience had come to fruition in September 1916 when stationed temporarily at the naval air base at Angernsee with a torpedo plane flight under his command. The flight had been shadowing a Russian fleet that had laid up in the Bay of Riga, but because the Russians had mined the sea around the bay so effectively none of the large German battleships or battle-cruisers could get close. The torpedo had just been created and trials had been carried out to some degree of success, so it was decided to use it against the Russian ships when possible.

On 12 September 1916 the Russian fleet moved out of the Bay of Riga and pairs of German reconnaissance aircraft searched for them. At 1730 hours, battleship *Slava*, escorted by six destroyers, was spotted steaming at full speed out of the bay. Edler gave the signal to attack and the seaplanes swept down. The Russian guns opened fire, covering the sky with exploding shells, and almost immediately the seaplanes dropped their torpedoes toward the battleship. As luck would have it one of the destroyers slid in front of the battleship, screening it from the torpedoes and was hit. The destroyer sank almost immediately. For his part in leading the raid Oberleutnant zur See Edler was awarded Knight 2nd Class with Swords of the White Falcon Order from the Grand Duchy of Saxe-Weimar-Eisenach. After his promotion to Kapitänleutnant in 1917, Edler was awarded another medal, the Wilhelm Ernst War Cross.

There has always been some dispute over whether a torpedo was actually used against the Russians in the Bay of Riga. Some historians believe that the torpedo was never used against the battleship *Slava* but that she was bombed – an allegation that can probably never be proved.

The mainstay fighter of the German Naval Air Service was the Hansa–Brandenburg W.29 monoplane which was faster, more manoeuvrable and more heavily armed than the Allied seaplanes. If attacked by Allied landplanes, however, the Hansa-Brandenburgs were disadvantaged because of the drag of their twin floats which restricted their speed and manoeuvrability in comparison. To combat the Allied seaplane threat, the German High Command ordered the production of a single-seater seaplane fighter scout aircraft (*Jagdeinsitzer Wasser*), to be used solely as an interceptor. The first fighter to make an appearance was the Brandenburg KDW, a converted scout, followed by the Rumpler 6B-I developed from the C.I and

Friedrichshafen at Kiel-Holtneau being prepared for take off.

Rumpler 6B-II, and the Albatros W.4. The Albatros W.4 was often thought to have been a converted D.I but, in fact, although the fuselage was basically the same as the D.I the remainder of the aircraft was considerably larger. The wing span was one metre longer and the tailplane had an increased area. The first of these aircraft was delivered in September 1916.

One aircraft that was used as torpedo-bomber was the twin-engined Brandenburg GW. Operating out of Seeflugstation Flandern I (Zeebrugge), the role of these aircraft was to attack enemy shipping in the English Channel with torpedoes. According to one German observer who flew on the missions in 1916, they were only used about five times because they could only operate when the weather was calm, and the only success recorded was that of a transport ship, which was sunk more by luck than judgement. None of the early naval aircraft were equipped with bombing equipment and any bombing was done by dropping 11lb bombs over the side of the aircraft. The subjects for the majority of the attacks were submarines, and although there are no recorded sinkings, a number were damaged, preventing them from submerging.

Navigation of naval aircraft at that time was carried out using a drawing compass and triangle and a drift meter. Small sea maps – 13.5in x 9.5in – derived from the large ones used on warships, were sectioned off into quadrants that showed the positions of mines, sunken vessels and buoys. Because these maps were top secret they were carried in specially made lead cases, so that in the event of the aircraft having to ditch into the sea, they could be thrown overboard to prevent them falling into enemy hands.

While inroads were being made into naval aviation in Europe, in the South Pacific and Indian Ocean, the German commerce raider *Wolf* was also making her presence felt with the use of an aircraft. The *Wolf*, which was disguised as a merchantman, was responsible for the capture of fourteen merchant ships – the majority of them with the help of the seaplanes she carried. When a ship was sighted, the seaplane, a Friedrichshafen FF.33e, *Wölfchen* ('wolf cub'), would take off and drop a warning bomb in front of the ship. If the ship did not heave to and allow a boarding party aboard, the aircraft would touch down on the water alongside

Friedrichshafen FF.29 at Kiel-Holtneau.

Freidrichshafen FF.33l on coastal patrol.

the vessel and hold the ship up at gun point. The latter happened to the American ship *Winslow*. Allied warships hunted high and low for the raider all over the Indian Ocean, so not only was the *Wolf* inflicting serious damage to the commercial shipping lanes, but was also tying up the warships who were hunting her. She finally returned to Germany with the little aircraft nicknamed *Wölfchen* proudly displayed on her deck. During her time at sea *Wölfchen* made more than fifty flights.

The appointment of Admiral Reinhardt Scheer on 23 February 1916 to command the German High Seas Fleet gave an unexpected boost to the German Naval Air Service inasmuch as Scheer was a great supporter of aviation recognising their potential. In an effort to lure British Admiral Robert Beatty's battle fleet from their base at Rosyth, Scheer planned a bombardment on the town of Sunderland. Submarines were to lay mines off the British bases, whilst Naval airships carried out reconnaissance missions. The battlecruisers, under the command of Admiral Franz von Hipper, would carry out the bombardment whilst the main body of the fleet would be waiting in the middle of the North Sea. The moment the British Fleet moved from its bases, their positions and any other relevant information would be relayed from the airships to the High Seas Fleet.

The attack was scheduled for 19 May, so on 15 May, fifteen submarines set sail to take up their positions. Problems with repairs to the battlecruiser *Seydlitz* caused the sailings of the main fleet to be delayed until 29 May. It was realised that the submarines would be at the limit of their endurance by 1 June. On 31 May the airship commander Peter Strasser ordered five of his Zeppelins to lift off and head for the British coast. Unfortunately for Scheer, British naval intelligence intercepted the radio messages and had broken the code so were well aware of all that was going on.

As the airships lifted off the adverse winds that had suddenly sprang up persisted and caused the airships to struggle against them. Admiral Scheer had set sail in the meantime, but the

Friedrichshafen FF.49c being hoisted aboard one of the German seaplane carriers, possibly the SMS Santa Elena.

airships had barely left the German coast and were no way near of being in position. By the morning of 1 June the five airships had returned to their base, though five replacement airships had lifted off early that morning. Even before dawn had broken the German High Seas Fleet was under attack and the information being relayed back by the Zeppelins was erratic and misleading to say the least. One report from the L.24 stated that they had spotted the main part of the British Fleet off northern Denmark and had bombed part of it. It has never been discovered what they saw or what they say they bombed, but it was certainly not the British Fleet as it was nowhere near the area at the time. This information had also been passed back to Admiral Scheer with the German High Seas Fleet, leading Scheer to believe that the British Fleet had settled there for the night.

Another airship, the L.11, sent back more reliable information, but even then their navigation was miles out. The airship suffered some minor damage from gunfire, from various escort destroyers, but nothing serious. At 0608 hours on 1 June, Scheer signalled Strasser to recall his airships as he no longer required them. The realisation that the main body of the British Fleet was so close to him caused Scheer to rethink his position in the face of almost overwhelming odds. The battle started and a number of ships were sunk and damaged on both sides, but the overwhelming superiority of the British Fleet caused the German High Seas Fleet to retreat.

The Battle of Jutland has filled many books and it is not the intention of the author to explore this battle in any depth, save to point out the limited use of aerial observation in such a battle.

Unlike their fellow army fliers, naval aircrew rarely came to the public's notice nor in fact the High Command, one such person was Leutnant zur See Wolfram Eisenlohr. One of six brothers who were equally spread between the army and the navy, Eisenlohr joined the navy and applied for a transfer to naval aviation. Out of all those who applied for flight training, he was the only one singled out to be an observer. Passing out from his course with flying colours, Eisenlohr, although hugely disappointed at not becoming a pilot, threw himself into his new position with enthusiasm.

Transferred to Seeflugstation Windau in May 1917, he carried out a number of reconnaissance flights, bombing missions and mine-laying flights. Then on 22 August 1917, Eisenlohr and his pilot were one of three Friedrichshafen FF.41a seaplanes sent to attack the stranded Russian torpedo-boat *Stroini*. The boat had run aground west of Zerel in the Baltic and frantic efforts had been made to free her. The first two aircraft made their bombing runs without success, then came Eisenlohr's turn and his bombs struck home. The damage caused by his bombs was enough for the Russians to abandon all attempts of salvaging the *Stroini* and left her to the elements. All Eisenlohr received for the sinking of a torpedo-boat was a small trophy from his fellow aviators. If that had been an army pilot any number of awards would have come his way.

On a second occasion, during a reconnaissance mission in the middle of a Russo-German naval battle, Eisenlohr and his pilot came across a lifeboat adrift in the open sea with one officer and seven sailors aboard. Ordering the pilot to land alongside them, Eisenlohr threw them a line and towed the boat for over an hour before reaching the German cruiser, SMS *Augsburg*. The tired and exhausted sailors were taken aboard to safety, most probably to be grateful prisoners of war. No recognition was given for this lifesaving act but he was later awarded the Bavarian Military Merit Cross and the Bavarian Silver Merit Medal.

Another of those rare breed of naval pilots who managed to capture the public's imagination, was Leutnant der Reserve der Matrosenartillerie (Lieutenant of Reserve of Naval Artillery) Theo Osterkamp who was to become the Imperial German Navy's top fighter pilot. Osterkamp joined the navy on 14 August 1914 with the express purpose of becoming a pilot. The story is, that Osterkamp arrived at Johannisthal outside Berlin expressing an interest in becoming a pilot, and when asked what his profession was, he replied, 'Forest Ranger.' 'In that case you are a natural observer', came the reply, and reluctantly Osterkamp

Three Friedrichshafen FF.41a seaplanes on the slipway at the Naval Air Station Windau.

accepted. Completing his training in March 1915, Osterkamp was posted to Wilhelmshaven on 24 March and almost immediately joined II Marine Feldflieger-Abteilung where he remained until 22 September 1915. During this time he carried out reconnaissance flights and bombing missions. Promoted to Vizeflugmeister in September 1915 and awarded the Iron Cross 2nd Class, he was posted to I Marine Feldflieger-Abteilung. On 6 September 1916 he claimed the shooting down of an enemy aircraft. It was confirmed by both his pilot and ground personnel. For some unknown reason this was not accepted by the authorities, but he was awarded the Iron Cross 1st Class the same month. His wasn't the only claim not to be accepted by the authorities, a fellow observer Oberleutnant Helmut Schmidt-Köppen also submitted a claim and that too was supported by ground troops, but rejected.

During his time as an observer Osterkamp carried out over 300 missions – among them a number of extremely dangerous ones. Then on 10 March 1917 he realised his ambition when he was accepted for pilot training and sent to Johannisthal for his basic flight training. Many months before he had persuaded his pilot, Leutnant Wilhelm Mattheus, to teach him the rudiments of flying, so on his first flight his instructor realised that his new pupil could already handle the aircraft and all he had to teach him to do was to land and take-off. Osterkamp sailed through the course in record time and on 13 April he reported to a new all-fighter detachment designated I Marine Land Feld Jagdstaffel under the command of Leutnant zur See Gotthard Sachsenberg. Osterkamp had been trained on old rotary-engined aircraft, but the new fighter detachment had the latest Albatros D.II and D.III fighters, which were a totally different aircraft altogether. Struggling to master the landing of the Albatros resulted

Royal visit by Kaiserin Augusta Victoria to Naval Air Station Holtenhau.

Kaiserin Augusta Victoria with her Lady-in-Waiting Baroness von Bredlow on a visit to the Naval Air Station Holtenhau. The officers, from left to right: Kapitänleutnant Günther Pluschow, Großadmiral Prinz Heinrich of Prussia and Fregattenkapitän Hermann Buchholz.

in Osterkamp being left out of all front line missions while he continued to practice. On one such practice flight he intercepted a British aircraft and shot it down. Harsh words were said to have been exchanged between Osterkamp and Sachsenberg regarding the fact that Osterkamp had 'strayed' toward the front line during this practice flight, but it was quickly realised that he was an exceptional pilot.

In the summer of 1917 a naval *Jagdgeschwader* ('fighter squad') was formed under the command of Leutnant Sachsenberg. Osterkamp was chosen as his deputy and to lead one of the three flights that made up the unit, II Mar. Felfjasta – a position he held for the remainder of the war. By August 1917 Osterkamp had raised his tally of victories to five and was awarded the Knight's Cross with Swords to the Hohenzollern House Order. In June 1917 Osterkamp's friend Mattheus had been posted to the *Jagdgeschwader*. The two continued to increase their tallies, but on 28 December 1917, Mattheus was shot and wounded during a dog-fight with British fighters; he died three days later.

In April 1918 both Sachsenberg and Osterkamp were awarded the 1st and 2nd Class Oldenburg Friedrich August Cross and later the Knight 1st Class with Swords of the Ducal House Order of Albert. By the end of July 1918, Sachsenberg had raised his tally to sixteen and was awarded the coveted Orden Pour le Mérite. Osterkamp had raised his tally to sixteen some months earlier, but because he was a reserve officer and Sachsenberg was a regular Sachsenberg was given preference. However the following month Osterkamp received his Orden Pour le Mérite and the two of them continued to raise the units tally.

Things did not always go so well – in one incident Osterkamp in his Fokker D.VII spotted a reconnaissance aircraft over Bruges. He fired a short burst into the aircraft and watched as

Oberleutnant Christiansen deep in conversation with aircraft designer Ernst Heinkel and an unknown civilian.

it slowly went into a spin – displaying the large German crosses beneath its wings. Osterkamp had attacked a Rumpler C.VII from a photographic squadron, he discovered later. Fortunately the pilot managed to carry out an emergency landing although the observer was slightly injured. Many years later Osterkamp met the observer and treated him to champagne.

Osterkamp ended the war with a total of thirty victories and went on to serve in the Luftwaffe during the Second World War. He died in 1985. One of the commanders of the Flanders base was Leutnant zur See Erich Killinger. Killinger had, up to this point in time, had one of the most exciting careers of any German naval officer. Born in Heidelberg in 1893, Killinger had joined the navy in 1912 and when war broke out was serving on board SMS *Berlin* as a Fähnrich zur See (Second Lieutenant). Bitten by the aviation bug he applied to join the aviation wing of the navy and was sent to the Marine Luftflieger-Abteilung school at Johannisthal just outside Berlin. After completing his course he was posted to the naval air station at Putzig in the Eastern Baltic, where he joined the ship SMS *Glyndwr* as a reconnaissance and bombing observer.

During a bombing mission on 6 April 1915 on the Russian bastion of Libau, his Rumpler aircraft was shot down by Russian ground fire. Both he and his pilot were captured and imprisoned in the Peter and Paul Fortress in St Petersburg. After lengthy interrogation, Killinger was inexplicably sentenced to death. One can only assume that as a bomb aimer on the raid he accounted for a large number of Russian troops and this was their way of exacting revenge for their deaths. The sentence was later commuted one of life imprisonment and Killinger was sent to a Siberian prison camp; it is not known what happened to his pilot. During the journey to the camp, Killinger managed to slip his guards and made his way back to Germany via China, Japan, United States, Norway and Sweden – taking over six months to complete the epic journey.

On his return Killinger found that in his absence he had been promoted to Leutnant zur See and awarded the Knight's Cross 2nd Class with Swords of the Zähringen Lion Order. After leave he was posted to Seeflugstation Flandern I at Zeebrugge on 26 July 1916 as a seaplane pilot. Within days of taking up his new post he intercepted three British aircraft attacking a German submarine and drove them off and for this he was awarded the Iron Cross 1st Class. During the following year more honours were heaped upon Killinger, including the Oldenburg Friedrich August Cross 1st and 2nd Class and Hanseatic Crosses from Hamburg and Lübeck. He was also recommended for the Württemberg Gold Military Merit Medal but was never awarded. The reason given at the time, was that Killinger did not come from Württemberg and therefore was not entitled to it.

At the beginning of 1918 Killinger was appointed to *I Adjutant des Gruppenkommandeurs der Seeflieger der Marinekorps und Frontflieger bei Seeflugstation Flandern I* (First Adjutant of the Group Commander of Seaplane Fliers of the Naval Corps and Frontline Fliers at Naval Air Station Flanders I). Just before the end of the war Killinger was awarded the Knight's Cross with Swords of the Royal House Order of Hohenzollern and Knight's Cross of the Military Karl Friedrich Merit Order.

Another of the German aviators who grabbed the headlines at the beginning of the war, Kapitänleutnant Günther Plüschow, known also as 'The Flier of Tsingtao'. Plüschow, then a Leutnant zur See, had been sent to China together with another naval pilot, Friedrich Müllerskowski and their aircraft, two Rumpler Taubes, to support 600 German marines who had landed and captured the city of Tsingtao. The attack was a retaliation after the murder of two German missionaries in the Shantung Province, but was also an excuse for Kaiser Wilhelm II to expand his colonial territories. On 4 August 1914, word reached Tsingtao that Germany and Britain were at war. Two weeks later a combined British-Japanese fleet blockaded the port and Japanese soldiers, supported by four Maurice Farman floatplanes landed on the shore at Tsingtao. The German garrison under the command of Kapitän zur See Alfred Meyer-Waldeck held out until 7 November 1914 and then surrendered.

A Friedrichshafen FF.41a 100 seaplane on the launching jetty at Naval Air Station Windau in 1917.

A Rumpler seaplane at the Naval Air Station Putzig. Leutnant zur See Killinger was shot down whilst flying this aircraft after which he made his dramatic escape from a prisoner-of-war camp.

Plüschow took to the air and headed for neutral China but had to crash-land as the engine had run out of fuel. Placed under arrest he was told that he was to be interned, but he escaped to Shanghai where he boarded a boat for America. On reaching America he changed his identity and stole aboard a cargo ship headed for Naples, Italy. He was stopped in Gibraltar when the the boat stopped to drop off supplies and was arrested. Identified as a German naval officer he was taken as a prisoner-of-war to Donnington Hall near Derby, England. One month later he made a daring escape and smuggled himself aboard a Dutch merchant ship headed for Holland. He returned to Germany at the end of July 1915 a hero, and was promoted to Oberleutnant zur See then posted to the Seeflugstation Libau near Riga. On 17 October 1915 he was promoted to Kapitänleutnant zur See and awarded both the 1st and 2nd Class Iron Cross, the Bavarian Military Merit Order 4th Class with Swords and from his home state of Mecklenburg-Schwerin the Military Merit Cross 2nd Class. Two months later he was awarded the Knight's Cross with Swords of the Royal House Order of Hohenzollern followed by the Order of the Zöhringen Lion Knight 2nd Class with Swords and Oakleaves. Gunther Plüschow commanded a number of seaplane stations throughout the war and died in 1931 in an air crash in South America.

In Europe there was one unit that consisted of two seaplane squadrons that operated out of List auf Sylt (Flanders), under the command of Leutnant Becht and Kapitänleutnant Friedrich Christiansen who had overall command of the unit. All seaplanes, with the exception of *Wölfchen*, flew from bases along the coast and although their role was more reconnaissance they were involved with a number of skirmishes with Allied fighters from time to time. Kapitänleutnant Friedrich Christiansen accounted for twenty-one aircraft and one airship. This is quite a remarkable score considering that most of the aerial combat was taking place over the front lines inland.

Duration of flights was limited to the amount of fuel carried and the fighters had a maximum duration of around three hours, whilst the larger Friedrichshafen was capable of staying aloft for over six hours on reconnaissance missions. Kapitänleutnant Christiansen's

No.1 seaplane squadron were on patrol off Flanders on 11 December 1917, when they came across the British semi-rigid airship C.27 on anti-submarine patrol. The squadron attacked with incendiary bullets and within minutes the airship was ablaze and plunging into the North Sea. All of the C.27's crew perished.

The conversion of a light cruiser to a seaplane-carrier in early 1918, showed the rapid progression of German naval aviation but conversely also the desperate straits that Germany found herself in. An additional seaplane-carrier had been requested by the High Seas Fleet so that more aerial reconnaissance could be carried out. An earlier report that had assessed the work carried out by converted merchantmen strongly recommended the building of a purpose-built aircraft carrier that was capable of carrying in excess of eight aircraft. Although accepted by the Naval High Command it was ruled that the building of such a vessel would take too long. Work on the light cruiser *Stuttgart* started in January 1918 and was finished in May 1918. The hangar built on her deck was capable of housing two Freidrichshafen 33 seaplanes whilst a third was carried on the deck. On joining the North Sea Aerial Force she became the flagship of Admiral Franz von Hipper and carried out minesweeping operations. At the end of the was she was surrendered to the British and taken to Teignmouth where she stayed until she was scrapped in 1920.

On 6 July 1918, five Hansa-Brandenburg seaplanes of No.1 squadron from Flanders seaplane station, led by Kapitänleutnant Christiansen, were on patrol when they surprised the British submarine C-25 on the surface off Harwich. The five seaplanes attacked the C-25 one after the other, raking it with machine-gun fire, and damaged it to the extent that it could not dive. Radioing back to their base at Flanders, the No.2 squadron took off to relieve No.1 squadron and found the C-25 submarine being towed by another British

The Coastal airship C.27 falling in flames after being shot down by Oberleutnant Friedrich Christiansen flying a Brandenburg floatplane.

submarine, the E-51. As soon as the E-51 commander saw the German seaplanes he severed the tow-rope and dived, leaving the C-25 to manage as best she could. Then No.2 squadron dropped ten 22lb bombs and severely damaged the C-25. The C-25 was claimed to have been sunk, but in fact it managed to make port after the seaplanes had been driven off by the destroyer HMS *Lurcher*, which then towed the stricken submarine into Harwich.

During the month of July, Christansen's squadrons accounted for three Curtiss flying boats and two Short seaplanes, but it wasn't without danger. One such incident at the beginning of the year was when one of the seaplanes based at Zeebrugge failed to return from a mission. A reconnaissance flight by Leutnant Becht, CO of 2nd C-Staffel, one of three squadrons based at Zeebrugge, the missing pilot was spotted in the water. Leutnant Becht landed nearby and taxied over to the pilot who clambered aboard one of the floats, holding on to the struts – the aircraft returned safely. Some months later Christiansen himself was involved in a similar rescue at the mouth of the Thames Estuary when he picked up two crew members of his squadron and brought them back. This method of rescuing downed crew members was adopted by the crews of the seaplanes and a number of fliers were saved in this fashion.

Not all crew members were rescued by their comrades. One such incident happened on 10 May 1918, when two Friedrichshafen FF.49c seaplanes were swung out from the deck of the seaplane-carrier *Santa Elena* to carry out a reconnaissance patrol and to map a minefield they had discovered earlier that week. One of the aircraft flown by Feldwebel Hans Sommermann (pilot) and his observer Feldwebel Georg Pätzold was to be involved in a dramatic incident and the crew only survived because of the ruggedness of their aircraft.

On reaching the minefield and mapping it, the two aircraft headed back for the *Santa Elena*. After more than six hours in the air and the seaplane-carrier nowhere in sight, the two seaplanes alighted on the water sending out SOS calls as they did so. Both aircraft put out sea anchors and waited for help to arrive. During the night a gale sprang up and one of the aircraft lost its sea anchor and it drifted away. Later the same night Sommermann and Pätzold lost their sea anchor and were left drifting helplessly in the North Sea. With no food or water, although there was water mixed with glycerine in the radiator, their situation became desperate. Relying solely on rainwater the now battered aircraft drifted across the storm-tossed sea. After five days the crew spotted some fishing vessels and fired red Very lights, but these were ignored. On the sixth day Pätzold ripped a piece of spar off the wing and attached a large white cloth to it. The skipper of a Swedish fishing smack *Argo II* saw the signal and moved alongside and took the crew off. He told Sommermann and Pätzold that had seen the red lights but interpreted them as a signal to keep away.

The two aircrew members had been adrift for more than a week and when they returned to Germany it was estimated that they and their aircraft had drifted for 140 hours and travelled almost twice across the North Sea. The crew members of the other seaplane had also been rescued by fishermen, who they had attracted by firing their machine gun in SOS bursts.

At the beginning of October 1918, orders came to evacuate all the seaplane bases along the coast and the pilot to be assigned to landbased squadron on reconnaissance duties. Within the month the whole of the German Army was in disarray when it was discovered the Kaiser Wilhelm II had fled to Holland.

At the end of the war the German Naval Air Service had thirty-two seaplane stations and bases in Flanders and the Baltic Sea, Turkey and the Balkans, and four seaplane-carriers ships. This did not include the twenty-six land flying units, over half of which were stationed in Flanders.

Top: *The British submarine C.25 caught on the surface by German floatplanes.*
Middle: *C.25 under attack from German Hansa-Brandenburg W.29 fighter aircraft of Christiansen Staffel. Note the splashes made by machine gun bullets just in front of the submarine.*
Bottom: *C-25 being bombed by Hansa-Brandenburg W.29 fighters. As can be seen by the eruptions around the submarine, their aim was not that good.*

The Felixstowe flying boat burning on the sea after being attacked by the Hansa-Brandenburg W.29 seaplane.

The SMS Glyndwr *with one of her aircraft on deck.*

Aircraft of the Imperial German Naval Air Service

	No. Built	Date in Service		No. Built	Date in Service
Ago C.I.W.	(1)	1915	Brandenburg W.29	(78)	1918
Ago C.II.W.	(2)	1915	Brandenburg W.32	(3)	1918
Albatros W.1	(5)	1915	Brandenburg W.33	(26)	1917
Albatros W.2	(1)	1916	Brandenburg W	(27)	1914
Albatros W.3	(1)	1916	Brandenburg LW	(1)	1916
Albatros W.4	(118)	1916	Brandenburg NW	(32)	1915
Albatros W.5	(5)	1917	Brandenburg GNW	(16)	1915
Albatros W.8	(2)	1917	Brandenburg KW	(3)	1916
			Brandenburg GW	(26)	1916
Brandenburg KDW	(58)	1916	Brandenburg GDW	(1)	1916
Brandenburg W.11	(2)	1916	Brandenburg CC	(26)	1916
Brandenburg W.12	(140)	1917	Brandenburg FB	1915	1915
Brandenburg W.16	(3)	1916			
Brandenburg W.17	(2)	1917	Friedrichshafen FF.29	(8)	1914
Brandenburg W.18	(1)	1917	Friedrichshafen FF.29a	(8)	1914
Brandenburg W.20	(3)	1917	Friedrichshafen FF.31	(2)	1915
Brandenburg W.19	(55)	1918	Friedrichshafen FF.33e/h/j/l		
Brandenburg W.25	(1)	1917		(135)	1916
Brandenburg W.26	(3)	1917	Friedrichshafen FF.34	(1)	1915
Brandenburg W.27	(1)	1917	Friedrichshafen FF.35	(1)	1915

Kapitänleutnant Günther Plüschow in his Friedrichshafen FF.33e.

	No. Built	Date in Service		No. Built	Date in Service
Friedrichshafen FF.37	(2)	1915	LG beck-Travemunde F.1 (3)		1914
Friedrichshafen FF.39	(14)	1915	LG beck-Travemunde F.2 (11)		1915
Friedrichshafen FF.40	(1)	1916	LG beck-Travemunde F.4 (34)		1917
Friedrichshafen FF.41	(9)	1916			
Friedrichshafen FF.43	(1)	1916	Oertz W 4	(2)	1914
Friedrichshafen FF.44	(1)	1916	Oertz W 5	(5)	1916
Friedrichshafen FF.48	(3)	1917	Oertz W 6 Flugschoner	(1)	1916
Friedrichshafen FF.49b	(25)	1917	Oertz W 7	(2)	1916
Friedrichshafen FF.49c	(14)	1917	Oertz W 8	(1)	1916
Friedrichshafen FF.53	(3)	1917			
Friedrichshafen FF.59a	(1)	1917	Rumpler 4B-11	(8)	1914
Friedrichshafen FF.59b	(1)	1917	Rumpler 4B-12	(18)	1915
Friedrichshafen FF.59c	(10)	1918	Rumpler 4E	(1)	1914
Friedrichshafen FF.60	(1)	1918	Rumpler 6B-1	(12)	1916
Friedrichshafen FF.63	(1)	1918	Rumpler 6B-2	(20)	1916
Friedrichshafen FF.64	(3)	1918			
			Sablatnig SF 1	(1)	1917
Gotha WD 1	(5)	1914	Sablatnig SF 2	(26)	1916
Gotha WD 2	(11)	1915	Sablatnig SF 3	(1)	1916
Gotha WD 3	(1)	1915	Sablatnig SF 4	(1)	1917
Gotha WD 5	(1)	1915	Sablatnig SF 5	(101)	1917
Gotha WD 7	(8)	1916	Sablatnig SF 7	(3)	1917
Gotha WD 8	(1)	1915	Sablatnig SF 8	(37)	1918
Gotha WD 9	(1)	1916			
Gotha WD 11	(13)	1917	Zeppelin-Lindau (Dornier) Rs I		
Gotha WD 12	(1)	1917		(1)	1915
Gotha WD 14	(69)	1917	Zeppelin-Lindau (Dornier) Rs II		
Gotha WD 15	(2)	1917		(1)	1915
Gotha WD 20	(3)	1917	Zeppelin-Lindau (Dornier) Rs III		
Gotha WD 22	(2)	1918		(1)	1917
Gotha WD 27	(3)	1918	Zeppelin-Lindau (Dornier) Rs IV		
Gotha Ursinus GUH	(1)	1916		(1)	1918
			Zeppelin-Lindau (Dornier) CS I		
Junkers J.11	(3)	1918		(1)	1918
			Zeppelin-Staaken Type `L' Seaplane		
K.W. (Kiel)	(3)	1917		(1)	1917
K.W. (Danzig)	(9)	1917	Zeppelin-Staaken Type 8301 Seaplane		
K.W. (Wilhelmshafen)	(6)	1917		(3)	1917
L.F.G. W	(1)	1917			
L.F.G. WD	(1)	1917			
L.F.G. Stralsund V19	(1)	1917			
L.T.G. SD1	(6)	1917			

The Friedrichshafen FF.33e Wölfchen *on the deck of SMS* Wolf *being prepared for a mission.*

A Hansa-Brandenburg GW seaplane initially designed to carry torpedoes but used primarily as a training aircraft.

The SMS Oswald *seen here with both her hangars furled and one of her seaplanes on deck being readied to go into the water.*

An Albatros W.5 carrying out torpedo trials at Friedrichshagen, near Berlin.

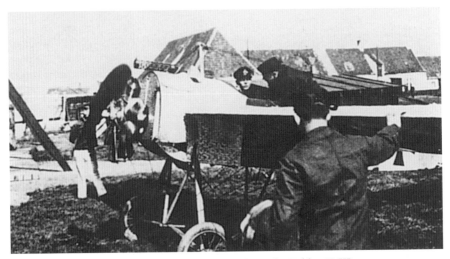

Leutnant zur See Gotthard Sachsenberg in the cockpit of a Fokker E.III.

Leutnant zur See Gotthard Sachsenberg standing in front of a new LVG.C.II of I. Marine Feldflieger-Abteilung, talking to some of his pilots.

Leutnant zur See Gotthard Sachsenberg when leader of I. Marine Feldflieger-Abteilung with pilots from his section.

A handwritten note from headquarters to Leutnant zur See Gotthard Sachsenberg telling him he had been awarded the Orden Pour le Mérite.

12
Austro-Hungarian Naval Air Service

The *Kaiserlich und Königlich Kriegsmarine* (Imperial and Royal Navy) Air Arm was the brain-child of Admiral Rudoph Graf Montecuccoli. Almost from its inception the air arm of the navy was in action as it took part in peace-keeping operations in Albania in 1913. All the Fregattenleutnant pilots were volunteers and gained a great deal of experience through these operations.

The interest in using an aerial device in combat was first mooted during the Austrian siege of Venice in 1849, when a number of unmanned hot-air balloons were sent aloft from the Austrian paddle steamer *Vulcano*. It is not recorded how they managed to make the balloons discharge their lethal load, but it made the *Vulcano* the first warship to use aerial devices in an offensive mode.

In 1911, an experimental air station was set up at Pola, from where reconnaissance training and exercises were carried out. During the First World War, Pola became the target of the US Naval Air Service which was stationed at Porto Corsini, Italy.

At the beginning of the First World War, the Austro-Hungarian air arm was amongst the most experienced of all the participants, but it lacked the funds to mount and sustain an extensive aerial campaign. They became increasingly reliant on the Germans for both finance and aircraft. This, of course, made them more and more dependent and beholden to the German military and, subsequently, more subservient.

During one operation on 22 July 1914, because the navy had no seaplane-carriers, the battleships *Herzog Franz Ferdinand*, *Radetzky* and *Zrinyi* each carried a Lohner flying boat from Pola to the Gulf of Cattaro. Once there they were lowered into the water to carry out reconnaissance flights over the Montenegrin border.

Compared to the aerial battles over the Western Front, there were very few aerial confrontations over the sea between the main fighting powers, mainly because they were over large expanses of water with few, if any, reference points. This was totally unlike those fighting over the land who had towns, front lines and other geographical landmarks to guide them. The difficulty of fighting over water was highlighted by the number of aircraft and aircrew lost during the war to aerial combat. The Austro-Hungarians lost three aircraft and three pilots in 1915, twelve aircraft and twenty pilots in 1916 and hardly any at all during the remainder of the war.

The first aerial attack over European waters was on the French armoured cruiser *Waldeck Rousseau*, by an Austro-Hungarian flying boat in the Adriatic on 17 October 1914 but it missed. The bombing of ships was not easy and the skill at this early point in the war had not been perfected. This is not too surprising considering aerial weapons were still in their infancy and most bombs were of an extremely crude design and manufacture.

There were some successes, however. On 16 August 1916, Austro-Hungarian seaplanes attacked and sank the British submarine B-10 at its moorings in Venice Harbour. Three weeks later Fregattenleutnant Maximillian Severa, the observer of a Lohner seaplane on a reconnaissance flight, spotted the French submarine *Foucault*, commanded by Lt de Vaisseau Leon Henri Devin, cruising just below the surface off Punta d'Ostro. The seaplane returned to its base at Cattaro where they learned that there were no 'friendly' submarines operating in the area. The commanding officer of the base, Linienschiffsleutnant Dmitri Konjovics, quick to spot an opportunity, displaced the original pilot but keeping the observer, Fregattenleutnant Severa, armed the aircraft with two 50kg depth charges and four smaller bombs, and took off after the submarine. A second aircraft similarly armed, flown by Fregattenleutnant Walter Zelezny and his observer Fregattenleutnant Otto Klimburg, accompanied Konjovics. On reaching the area in which the submarine was first spotted, the two aircraft adopted a search pattern and after thirty minutes spotted the submerged submarine in the clear water. Walter Zelezny brought his aircraft round and dived in to attack and dropped both his depth charges alongside the port side of the *Foucault*. The resulting explosion damaged the submarine's motor and stern glands, and caused the electrics to short circuit, starting a fire. Diving the submarine to 250ft, Devin put the fire out and tried to repair the motors, but to no avail. He decided to surface and fight it out with her deck gun. The two seaplanes had seen the submarine crash dive and the consequent ever-widening oil slick and circled the area. As the *Foucault* broke surface, once again it was Walter Zelezny who swept in to attack and dropped his four small bombs on to the conning tower. None of the bombs exploded, but Devlin realised that his boat was now a sitting duck and reluctantly ordered his crew on to the casing. They released carrier pigeons to inform their base of their situation and abandoned the submarine. Devlin opened all the main vents and waited until the submarine sank beneath him before actually leaving it. The two seaplanes landed and picked up Devin and his 1st Lieutenant and flew them to Cattaro; the remainder of the crew were picked up by the torpedo-boat 100-M and taken to the cruiser *Sankt Georg*. They were interned for the remainder of the war.

The Austro-Hungarian Naval Air Arm, like its counterpart in Germany, was overshadowed by the Army's air arm and had very few personalities who had the ability or the opportunity to stand out. There were only two Aces in the air arm of the Austro-Hungarian Navy, they were Linienschiffsleutnant (Lieutenant Commander) Gottfried Freiherr von Banfield and Fliegermeister Friedrich Lang. Born in 1890 in Castel Nuovo, on the Gulf of Cattaro, Gottfried Banfield was the son of a career naval officer in the Austro-Hungarian Navy, his destiny planned from that moment. He joined the Navy in 1905, graduated in 1909, and after

A Lohner S Type flying boat of the Austrian Navy flying over the cruiser Radetzky.

Hansa-Brandenburg flying boat A-24. Austro-Hungarian Ace Gottfried Banfield standing by the port wing.

spending several years at sea became fascinated with the world of aviation. He was selected to go for pilot training in Weiner-Neustadt in May 1912 and graduated in October 1912. He was awarded his *Feldpilotabzeichen* (Field Pilot's Badge) and almost immediately was sent to Paris with Linienschiffsleutnant Wosecek to test the new Leveque-designed flying boat. During one of the test flights on the Seine, Banfield had just taken off and was starting to climb when he realised that one of the many bridges that spanned the river was closer than he thought. Realising that he would be unable to get enough power to climb over the bridge, he throttled back and, skimming the water, flew under it – much to his immense relief. The following day the Paris newspapers bannered the headline: 'Austrian Dare-Devil Flies Under Seine Bridge.' The result of the test flying was that the Austro-Hungarian Naval Air Arm purchased two Donnet-Leveque flying boats with spare engines.

At the beginning of the war Banfield, together with two other pilots and their aircraft, was assigned to the cruiser SMS *Zrinyi* together with his Lohner flying boat E.21. On reaching the Gulf of Cattaro the aircraft were unloaded and then flown to Kumbor to carry out reconnaissance and artillery spotting for the fleet. Banfield's first recorded victory was on 27 June 1915 when he spotted an Italian observation balloon and fired some 500 rounds into it and destroyed it. The following day he dropped a bomb on an enemy position, and the explosion that followed indicated that he had actually hit an ammunition dump.

One of the most traumatic days in Banfield's career happened on 1 September 1915, when in the space of three hours he was involved in aerial combat with four different enemy aircraft and came very close to being shot down. Banfield, with his observer *Seekadett* Heribert Strobl Edler von Ravelsberg, had his first encounter with a Curtiss flying boat which they forced down with accurate gunfire. Less than half an hour later they were attacked by an Italian Macchi Type-L flying boat, but they managed to force it down. The Italian crew managed to re-start their engine and resumed the fight, only to be badly damaged in the ensuing fight forcing them to make an emergency landing into the sea. On their way back to base Banfield encountered another Italian flying boat and dived into the attack. This time he fired his

Pospesnyj *being towed into port after hitting a mine.*

machine guns until his ammunition was exhausted. Fortunately, so was his opponent's, who broke off the engagement and headed away. Nearing their base they were attacked again by an enemy flying boat and with some superb flying, and using their pistols and carbine, they managed to fend the enemy off. They were extremely lucky to survive.

In April 1916 Banfield took possession of a Lohner L.16 flying boat which had been specially modified and had a forward-firing machine gun mounted in front of the cockpit. Two days later he increased his tally to five and for this he was promoted to *Linienschifftsleutnant* (Lieutenant Commander) and given command of the Naval Air Station at Lloyd's Arsenal, Trieste.

Over the next two years Banfield increased his tally to nine – officially, but without doubt his tally was actually around twenty, and for this was awarded the *Ritterkreuz des Militär-Maria-Theresien-Ordens*.

The other naval aviator in the Austro-Hungarian Navy who became an household word was Fliegermeister Friedrich Lang. Lang started his naval career as a *Seefähnrich* (Naval Ensign) aboard the destroyer *Balaton* and while on board this vessel he received the Silver Bravery Medal 2nd Class. Quickly bored with the humdrum life aboard a small ship, he applied for a transfer to the Naval Air Service and was posted to the Naval Flier's School on the island of Cosada, which is situated at the southern tip of the Istrian Peninsula at the northern section of the Adriatic Sea. While there he was promoted to Fregattenleutnant and received his pilot's licence on 20 June 1916. After a brief spell at Kumbor he was posted to Durazzo where he flew reconnaissance missions and ship protection flights in the Lohner TI (L.131).

On one escort mission on 22 August 1916, Lang, with his observer *Einjährig-Freiwilliger* (volunteer) *Stabsmaschinenwärter* Franz Kohnhauser, intercepted six Farman biplanes on their way to attack the Naval Air Station at Durazzo. Diving into the formation, Lang and his observer raked the first of the Farmans with machine gun fire forcing it to ditch into the sea. A second Farman dived into attack and it too was forced to make an emergency landing on the sea. As they flew over the stricken aircraft, Lang noticed that the crew were wearing

French uniforms, but the Lohner TI had also suffered at the hands of the Farman's gunners and required some urgent repairs, forcing Lang to break off the engagement and head for home.

At the beginning of 1917, Lang was posted to the Naval Air Station at Pola where once again he was soon in the thick of the action. In May 1917 he was awarded the Military Merit Cross, 3rd Class, with War Decoration and Swords, and the Silver Military Merit Medal with Swords.

Because of the increased air attaacks on Pola, it was decided to operate a specialist fighter unit at an airfield called Altura just inland from Pola. A change of aircraft to Phönix D.I also created a change in fortune and the unit capitalised on it by attacking a formation of Italian reconnaissance aircraft and destroying two of the escort fighters.

Lang became an 'Ace' on 12 August 1918 when he shot down an Italian Macchi L-3 flying boat for which he was awarded a second Military Merit Cross, 3rd Class, with War Decoration and Swords. One month later he was awarded one of the highest honours – the Iron Crown, 3rd Class, with War Decoration and Swords. Lang finished the war with a total of nine victories and, like the quiet, reserved man that he was, faded into obscurity.

The Austro-Hungarian contribution to the first naval air war was relatively minor when compared to that of Germany and Britain, but nevertheless left its mark.

Austro-Hungarian Naval Aircraft of the First World War

Donnet-Lévêque flying boats

Fokker E.III

Hansa–Brandenburg Type A
Hansa–Brandenburg Type CC
Hansa–Brandenburg W.18 flying boats

Lohner Type L flying boat
Lohner Type M flying boat
Lohner Type TI flying boat
Lohner L-16

Paulham–Curtiss flying boats

Phönix D.I fighters

The British submarine B-10 in drydock in Venice after being raised after having been sunk during an Austrian air raid.

Lohner Type T flying boat L-47 of the Austro-Hungarian Navy after being captured by the Italians.

Shore crew ferry the pilot Fregattenleutnant Konstantin Maglic ashore at Kumbor in the southern Adriatic, summer 1914. His aircraft, the Lohner Type M, No.E-21, is being prepared to be brought ashore.

French-built Donnet-Leveque of KUK Kriegsmarine. The man in the leather coat with his back to the camera is Gottfried Banfield.

Gottfried Banfield stands up in the cockpit of his Lohner flying boat L-16, with his arm on the engine starter crank. Note the Schwarzlose M 7/12 machine gun fixed to the front deck.

Excellent shot of Gottfried Banfield at Trieste Naval Air Station in the summer of 1917.

An OEFFAG Type H flying boat at Trieste Naval Air Station. This aircraft was the only one of its type and was designed by Josef Mickl specifically for Gottfried Banfield.

Hansa-Brandenburg Type CC No. A-24 at Trieste Naval Air Station.

*The meeting of the Aces. Naval Ace Gottfried Banfield in the cockpit of a naval Phönix D.1.
Standing beside the aircraft is Army Ace Godwin Brumowski.*

Gottfried Banfield in the cockpit of his Hansa-Brandenburg A-11 at the Trieste Naval Air Station in 1917.

Lt de Vaisseau Leon Henri Devin, commander of the submarine Foucault, *and his observer, after being picked up from the water and taken to Pola. They are with the Austrian crew of the Lohner seaplane that sunk their submarine.*

The French submarine Foucault *which was sunk by Austro-Hungarian seaplanes. This was the first submarine to be sunk from the air.*

A Lohner L.50 about to lift off the water.

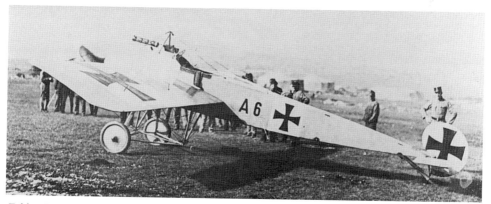

Fokker E.III NmQ.A-6 fitted with a Spandau machine gun. This aircraft was one of the fighters that was flown by Gottfried Banfield.

Hansa-Brandenburg W.18 flying boats of Banfield's squadron at Trieste Naval Air Station.

A Lohner S flying boat of the Austro-Hungarian Navy.

13
Photograph Gallery

North Sea Airship No. 4 of the RNAS, about to make her maiden flight. The semi-rigid airship envelope contained some 360,000 cubic feet of gas. The control car slung underneath was capable of carrying two crews.

The RNAS observer, Lt. York-Moore RN, seen here in a posed photograph showing how a bomb would be dropped from an airship.

A Fairey Campania about to be hauled up the slipway at Calshot after completing a test flight.

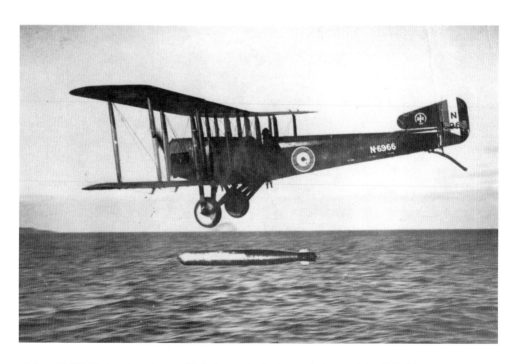

A Sopwith TI Cuckoo dropping an 18-inch torpedo during preliminary trials off Calshot.

Sopwith Tabloid No.394, powered by a 100hp Gnome and capable of 92mph.

An experimental Lewis gun mounting on a late production Sopwith Tabloid scout.

A Sopwith Pup, a graceful single seater fighter. It was first flown during the spring of 1916, and was sent to France for operational evaluation by RNAS pilots in May; it was praised for its speed and agility. It was armed with a .303 inch Vickers gun and a Pup flown by Flt. Sub-Lt. B.A. Smart from HMS Yarmouth downed naval Zeppelin L 23 on 1 August 1917.

Skids for deck landing trials on a Sopwith Pup, 15 April 1918.

The first produced Sopwith Triplane No.500 which was completed on 28 May 1916 and first flown by Harry Hawker. He is reported to have looped the aircraft within three minutes of lift-off. The Triplane had a great rate of climb and greatly impressed the RNAS pilots who put it through operational evaluation in June.

Sopwith Triplane prototype N500 of 'A' Squadron RNAS being prepared for its first test flight.

The Sopwith Triplane (N5350) prototype built by Clayton and Shuttleworth, with test pilot Harry Hawker about to carry out its first test flight.

Sopwith 1F1 Camel B384 'Wongo Bonga' of No.12 (N) Squadron in which Flt. Sub-Lt. Brandon shot down a Gotha bomber on 22 August 1917.

The end of a five-hour patrol.

A three-point landing in the sea.

The wreckage of what is believed to be a Sopwith Camel, being examined by German soldiers. The body of the pilot is visible on the left.

Lanchester Armoured Car No. 4 of 'A' Section, 15 Squadron RNAS.

Flt. Sub-Lt. Reginald Alexander John Warneford, VC. He made his name by downing Zeppelin LZ 37 over Ghent in Belgium, for which he was awarded the Victoria Cross. Only ten days later, on 17 June 1915, he was killed while flying a Henry Farman.

Flt. Sub-Lt. Raymond Collishaw, a Canadian who travelled to Britain to join the RNAS at his own expense. He went on to end the war with a total of 59 kills. He retired as an Air Vice Marshal in 1943.

Commander Charles Rumney Samson, DSO, RNAS being congratulated on his return from a bombing sortie, Imbros, Middle East, 1915. Aircraft is a Farman F.27.

Samson in the cockpit of a Nieuport 10, while operating from the island of Tenedos in 1915.

Harry George Hawker, an Australian who at one time held the British flying records for speed, altitude and endurance. He joined Sopwith in 1912 as a mechanic and became the flight test pilot for all Sopwith's machines. He also had influence over the designs of the 1 ½ Strutter, Pup, Triplane and Camel. He died in a flying accident in 1921.

A Short seaplane being refuelled.

A Short 184 seaplane dropping a torpedo.

A Short 184 setting off on patrol.

Short 310A seaplane dropping its torpedo during trials off Calshot, 1916.

A Short 310A seaplane dropping a torpedo, Calshot, 19 February 1918. Water can be seen splashing up to the underside of the plane, emphasising how risky the procedure could be.

Felixstowe F2A in an experimental black and white camouflage during trials.

Felixstowe F2A flying boats on the slipway at RNAS Killingholme waiting to be launched.

A Felixstowe F2A is towed on a lighter.

An FBA flying boat.

The US Naval Air Station at Arcachon, France.

The US Naval Air Station at Gujon, France.

Macchi M5 seaplanes of the US Navy on the slipway of the US Naval Air Station at Porto Corsini, Italy.

Ground crews hauling a Macchi M5 up the slipway at USNAS Porto Corsini.

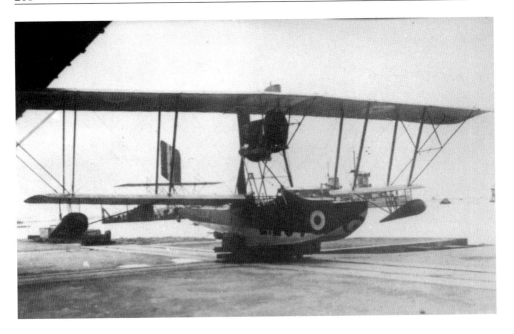

A Macchi L.2 flying boat outside its hangar ready to be placed on its beaching trolley for launching.

Medal of Honor winner Charles H. Hammann US Navy, in front of a Macchi M-8 flying boat at USNAS Porto Corsini.

Curtiss H-12 on the step about to take off.

Curtiss H-12 off the Scottish coast, 1917.

A Curtiss 'Large America' flying boat.

Prototype Caproni.

Prototype Caproni Ca5 floatplane during taxiing trials.

Caproni Ca43 on its beaching skids.

Lieutenant Commander Willis B. Haviland, Commanding Officer of USNAS Porto Corsini, standing by his Macchi M.5 No.31 with its distinctive 'flying goat' insignia.

Macchi M.5 of the USNAS taxiing along the the 70-foot wide canal towards the slipway at Porto Corsini.

Count Francesco Baracca, Italy's top ace, standing by his SPAD XIII fighter.

The seaplane carrier Almaz.

The Russian torpedo boat Stroini *aground in the Baltic where three F.F.41 seaplanes found her.*

The Russian seaplane carriers Alexsandr, Nikolai *and the Romanian ships* Romania *and* Regele Carol.

The German light seaplane carrier SMS Glyndwr, *a converted merchant ship built by Blohm & Voss, with Friedrichshafen seaplanes on deck.*

The German seaplane carrier Answald *seen here with canvas hangars amidships and aft.*

The German seaplane carrier SMS Santa Elena *with canvas hangars amidships and aft.*

A single-seater Albatros W.4 floatplane fighter, which entered service with the German Navy in late 1916. It was mostly used for local air defence of naval seaplane bases in the Flanders area.

Lohner E Type being hauled out of the water in harbour.

Lohner L Type No. L87.

Lohner L Type at moorings.

Lohner R Type recce flying boat No.38.

The Hansa-Brandenburg NW was the floatplane version of the Hansa-Brandenburg B1. Used as a re-connaissance aircraft during the First World War, it is seen here on its beaching trolley at NAS Zeebrugge.

Friedrichshafen FF.33L two-seater reconnaissance seaplane being hauled up the slipway at Mudros.

Austro-Hungarian Lohner reconnaissance plane shot down by a US Navy pilot off the coast of Venice, 1917.

Oberleutenant zur See Theodore Osterkamp, Commanding Officer of Marine Feldjasta II during the First World War, and holder of the prestigious Orden Pour le Mérite which can be seen around his neck.

Index